Pony Express

VOYAGE OF DISCOVERY™
The Story Behind the Scenery®

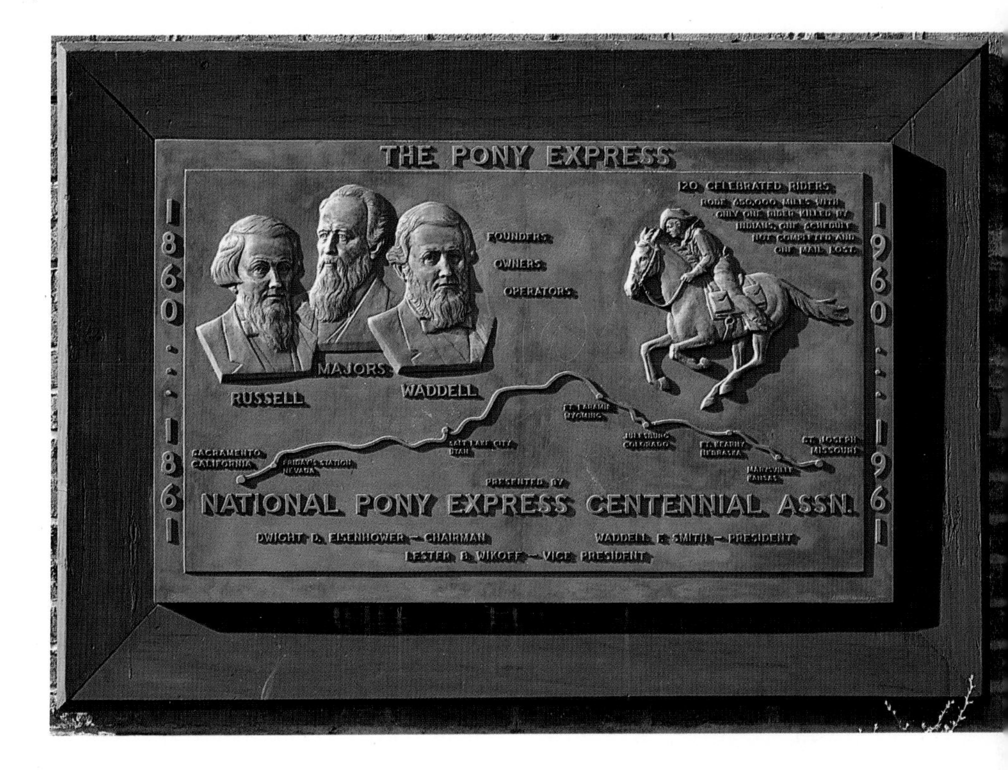

text
by
Anthony Godfrey
and Roy Webb

photography
by
Jeff Gnass

ANTHONY GODFREY, Ph.D., is the president of U.S. West Research, Inc., a public history and cultural resource management firm located in Salt Lake City, Utah. Trained in Native American and American Western history at the University of Utah, he has written, taught, lectured, and testified in court on these and related topics for the last 20 years.

ROY WEBB is an archivist in Special Collections, J. Willard Marriott Library, University of Utah. He has lived all his life in the West, and is the author of three books and numerous articles on the history of travel on the Colorado River, and other aspects of American Western history.

JEFF GNASS travels extensively throughout the continent photographing scenic and historic places, and documenting our heritage lands. Since first picking up a large-format camera in 1978, his images have graced thousands of pages in books, calendars, and magazines.

Front cover: Reenactment of Pony Express rider. Inside front cover: Home Station #1, St. Joseph, Missouri. Page 1: Pony Express Centennial Plaque. Page 4/5: Setting sun on the Missouri River.

Edited by Cheri C. Madison. Book design by Stuart Martin.

LC 99-60060. ISBN 0-88714-147-1.

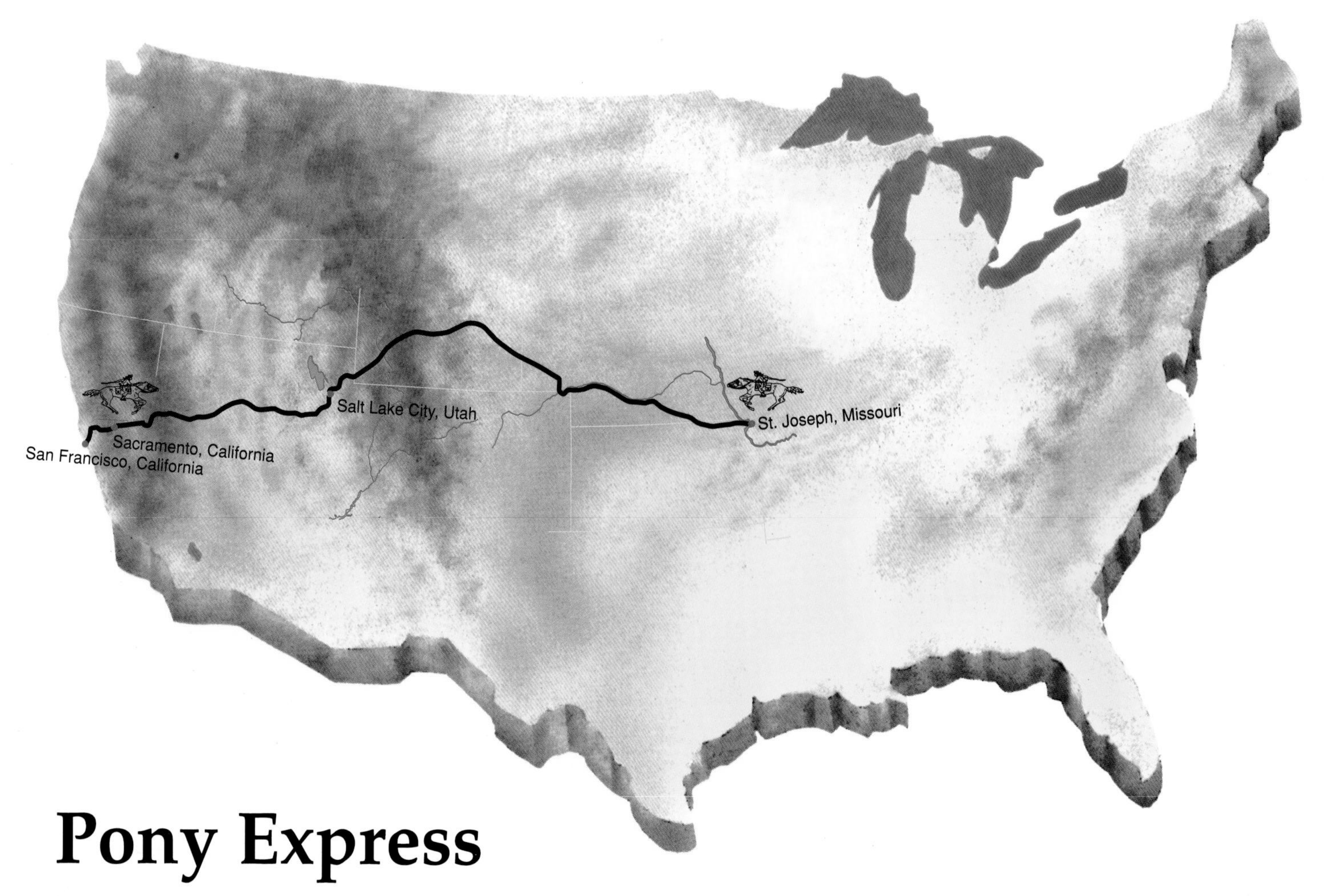

Pony Express

VOYAGE OF DISCOVERY

The idea of a pony express isn't a new one—the ancient empires that stretched across vast distances of Asia, Africa, and Europe had to have some way to transmit information as quickly as possible. Darius the Great of the Persian empire had a very efficient post-horse system that covered much of today's Middle East. Ancient Rome built great paved highways such as the Appian Way for the rapid and efficient transmittal by chariot or swift horses of military orders, dispatches, and important mail. In thirteenth-century China, Marco Polo reported that the Great Khan had stations for horse-carried mail a good day's ride apart, and used over 200,000 horses for his own pony express.

While the idea of a pony express is found in ancient times, Americans—that most practical of people—also put the idea to use well before 1860. Newspaper editors on the East Coast were using a post express to gather news and election returns as early as 1825, and General Stephen Watts Kearny, commander of the lands recently won from Mexico, established a semi-monthly courier service between San Diego and San Francisco by 1850. Marcus Whitman, the famous Oregon missionary, called for a relay system to carry mail between the "states" and the West Coast as early as the 1840s.

But when we think today of the Pony Express, we don't think of Kublai Khan or Marcus Whitman. No, we think of the riders of "the" Pony Express, those young men who galloped across the continent during the critical years of 1860 and 1861. The Pony Express was only in operation for about 18 months, and was never a financial success; indeed, the expenses incurred in operating the Pony Express, coupled with other reverses, spelled the end of the fortunes of the men who operated it. Yet few enterprises in American history have had such a hold on the popular imagination as the Pony Express, and interest in it continues to this day.

The Pony Express was brought about by the need for mail service in the burgeoning population centers of California, Utah, and Oregon. In 1845, a message from President James K. Polk took six months to go from Washington, D.C., to California. After the Mexican War added California to the United States, this was no longer acceptable. In 1849, the Gold Rush—combined with earlier migrations to Oregon and Utah—made America an empire with two coasts, albeit one with a big gap in the middle. Post offices were established in both Salt Lake City and San Francisco in the 1850s. Mail originally went by ship, from the coasts to Panama, where it was carried across the isthmus, then loaded onto another ship and taken to its destination. After the railroad across the isthmus was completed in 1855, this took about three weeks in good weather, although many ship-

"I, ____________, do hereby swear, before the Great and Living God, that during my engagement, and while I am an employee of Russell, Majors & Waddell, I will, under no circumstances, use profane language; that I will drink no intoxicating liquors; that I will not quarrel or fight with any other employee of the firm, and that in every respect I will conduct myself honestly, be faithful in my duties, and so direct all my acts as to win the confidence of my employers. So help me God."

Pledge of the C.O.C. and P.P. Express Company.

ments were delayed by bad weather and many were lost at sea. In 1851, overland mail service was established in two segments: California to Utah, and Utah to St. Louis. Though the men involved worked hard, the mail service was not effective for both physical and political reasons.

Physically, it was just a long way—almost 2,000 miles—from the edge of the frontier in Missouri to California. At the speed of a walking horse or a plodding team of oxen, that meant about three months on the trail. Other obstacles were high mountains, often choked with snow; long stretches of waterless desert; and the endless Plains, with their storms, swollen rivers, and hostile tribes. Politically, the sectional conflicts that would soon tear the nation apart affected even the far-off West. The government sent out surveyors to seek routes for overland mail and for the proposed railroad to the Pacific. Both sides agreed a northern route was impractical; but northerners naturally favored a central route, or in other words anyplace but through the southern states. Southerners, of course, wanted a southern route, through Texas, New Mexico, and Arizona to southern California and thence up the coast. Since they had enough power in Congress, and the support of President Buchanan, to decide which way the mails would go, that's the way the route went. Ben Holladay started the Overland Mail Service in 1857, and his stages took the southern route. It was long and it was hot, but the better weather along this route meant that the stages could run more frequently and with greater regularity, taking about 22 days to go from St. Louis to California.

Mail and passengers were also carried along the central route, following a trail established by John Hockaday and George Chorpenning, who had been working out routes and carrying passengers since 1851. But bad weather in the Sierra sometimes caused lengthy delays, and the stage could take a month or more to reach California. Chorpenning established a muleback mail service, called the "Jackass Mail," between Salt Lake City and the West Coast, but the first trip took 53 days instead of the promised 30. Obviously, something faster was essential. When gold was discovered at Pikes Peak in the Rocky Mountains in 1858, and in western Nevada that same year, the clamor for rapid mail service rose to a fever pitch.

Like so many legends, the actual origins of the Pony Express are clouded in half-truths and tall tales, and any number of individuals later claimed credit. One of the principal players was Senator William Gwin of California, who got the idea of a pony express while traveling on horseback from San Francisco to Washington in 1854. His companion for part of the way was Benjamin Ficklin, an employee of the Leavenworth and Pikes Peak Express Company. The firm was one of many owned by William Russell, of the freighting firm of Russell, Majors, and Waddell. The idea seems to have grown out of conversations the two men had along the trail. Then, during the winter of 1859, Gwin met William Russell in Washington, D.C., and suggested to him that if the time it took to communicate between California and the East were shortened, it might result in mail and passenger contracts, and a transcontinental railroad might even be built along the same route (as it eventually was). Senator Gwin hinted that if Russell could demonstrate the feasibility of such a route, he would use his influence to get a subsidy to help pay the expenses. Russell, always with an eye out for a good deal, jumped at the idea, reportedly without even asking his partners what they thought.

There are other versions of who first came up with the idea of the Pony Express, but at any rate, we know for sure that on January 27, 1860, three partners—William H. Russell, Alexander Majors, and William B. Waddell, who had experience in freighting all over the West, from Missouri to Santa Fe, Denver, and Salt Lake City—organized the Central Overland California and Pikes Peak Express Company, which was the official name of the Pony Express. Because of Russell's promises to start service in the spring, the three partners now had about 60 days in which to hire riders, station keepers, and stock tenders; purchase hundreds of horses and distribute them to the stations, many of which weren't built or even located yet; arrange for central offices and agents for the mail, in half a dozen widely separated locations; and purchase thousands of pounds of supplies, from hay to cartridges to sacks of flour, and likewise distribute them to the far-flung home and relay stations. It's easy to imagine Majors and Waddell muttering under their breaths about what their danged-fool partner had gotten them into this time.

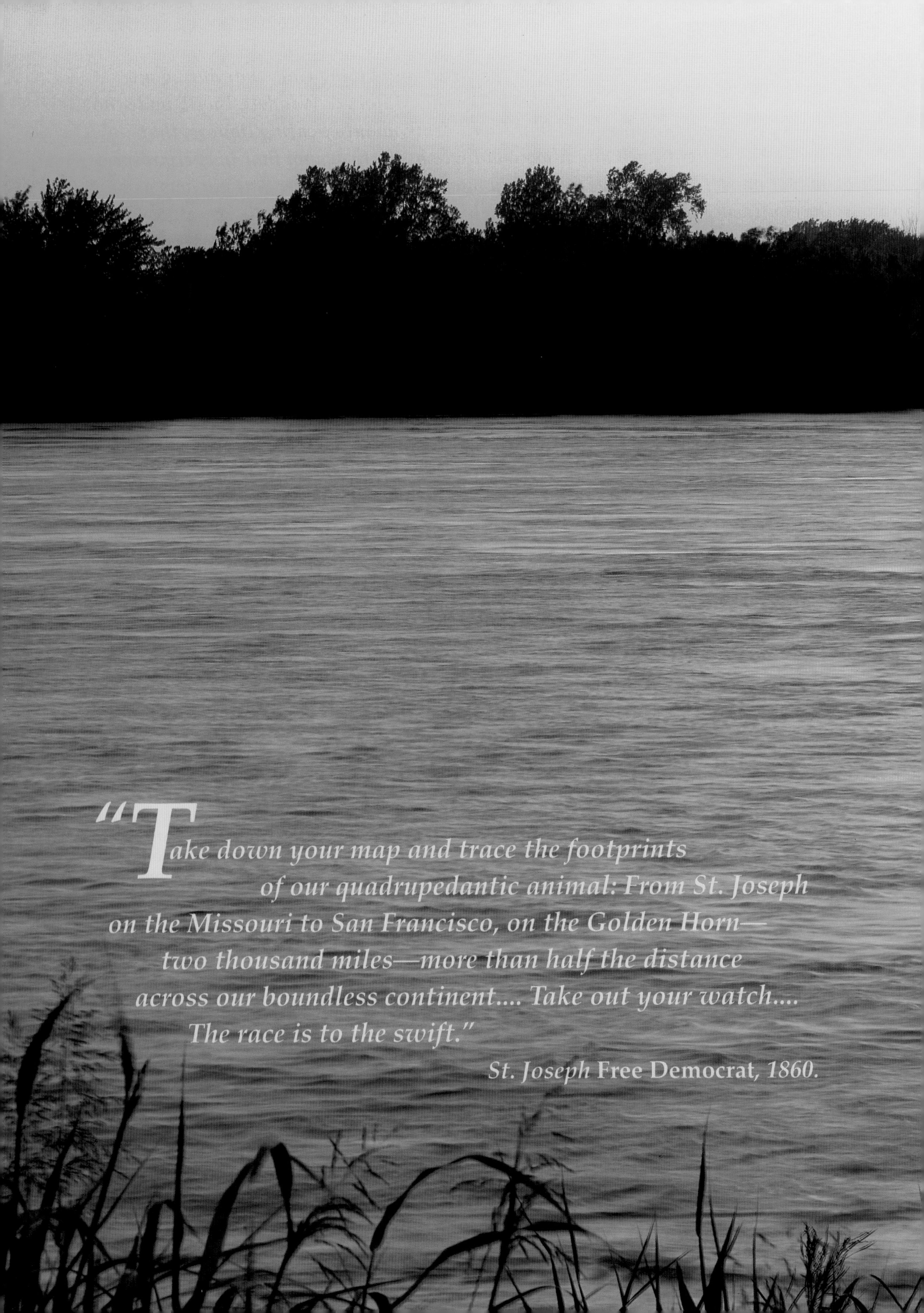
"Take down your map and trace the footprints
of our quadrupedantic animal: From St. Joseph
on the Missouri to San Francisco, on the Golden Horn—
two thousand miles—more than half the distance
across our boundless continent.... Take out your watch....
The race is to the swift."
St. Joseph Free Democrat, 1860.

PATEE HOUSE MUSEUM
1860
PONY
EXPRESS
OFFICE

"At 7 o'clock a.m., we were ordered from the stables two blocks east of the Patee House which was the signal for the ferry boat to come from Elwood and to lie in waiting at the landing until our arrival. We rode into the office and put on the mail, which consisted of four small leather sacks six by twelve inches, fastened onto a square holder which was put over the saddle.... When the mail was put on... [the rider] bounded out of the office door and down the hill at full speed, when the cannon was fired again to let the boat know that the pony had started..."

John Keetley.

April 3, 1860. Finally, after six weeks of frantic preparation, the day of the First Ride arrived. Announcements of the upcoming service had already been made in newspapers in California, Missouri, and New York. On the appointed day, great crowds gathered in both St. Joseph and Sacramento, bands played, salutes were fired, and local politicians, eager to be associated with this great enterprise, took the opportunity to make speeches.

With all the legends associated with the Pony Express, it's no surprise that the identity of the first rider from St. Joseph to Sacramento remains in doubt, although it's been narrowed down over the years to either Billy Richardson or Johnny Frye of Kansas. After a late start when the train from back east carrying the mail was delayed, the rider was off to salutes from cannon and brass bands. The mail reached Salt Lake City at 6:45 p.m. on April 9, 1860, and the rider immediately pressed on to Carson City, Nevada, arriving there on April 12. When the rider finally reached Sacramento two days later, the state legislature adjourned in honor of the great event, and the streets were filled with citizens eager to catch a glimpse of the valiant rider as he thundered past. The mail pouch was then given to the captain of the river steamer *Antelope*, which cast off at once for San Francisco. The first Pony Express pouch from east to west reached San Francisco about midnight, April 14, 1860, and the rider was taken off to a rowdy reception in his honor at the Newspaper Union Hall.

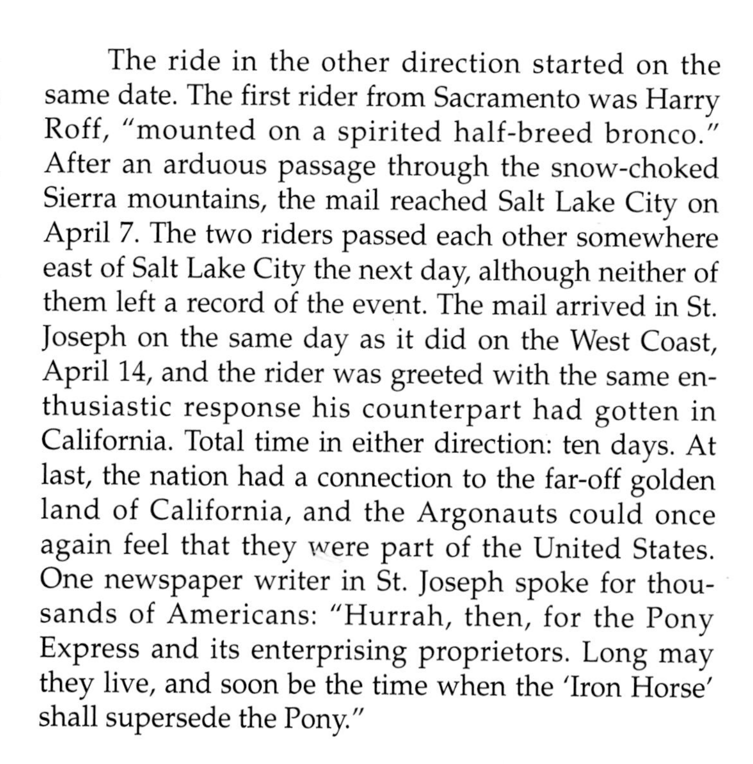

The ride in the other direction started on the same date. The first rider from Sacramento was Harry Roff, "mounted on a spirited half-breed bronco." After an arduous passage through the snow-choked Sierra mountains, the mail reached Salt Lake City on April 7. The two riders passed each other somewhere east of Salt Lake City the next day, although neither of them left a record of the event. The mail arrived in St. Joseph on the same day as it did on the West Coast, April 14, and the rider was greeted with the same enthusiastic response his counterpart had gotten in California. Total time in either direction: ten days. At last, the nation had a connection to the far-off golden land of California, and the Argonauts could once again feel that they were part of the United States. One newspaper writer in St. Joseph spoke for thousands of Americans: "Hurrah, then, for the Pony Express and its enterprising proprietors. Long may they live, and soon be the time when the 'Iron Horse' shall supersede the Pony."

The Patee House, where the Pony Express had its offices, was the height of luxury when it was opened by John Patee in 1858. It cost $180,000 and had 140 guest rooms, and William Russell and Alexander Majors, as well as riders and staff, often stayed there. During the Civil War it served as the Provost Marshall's office, and later was a girls' school and a shirt factory. Today, the Patee House is on the National Register of Historic Places.

The Pony Express stables are located just down the street from the Patee House. The stables were originally built by Ben Holladay in 1858 to serve his transportation business to Colorado. Today, the building houses the Pony Express Museum.

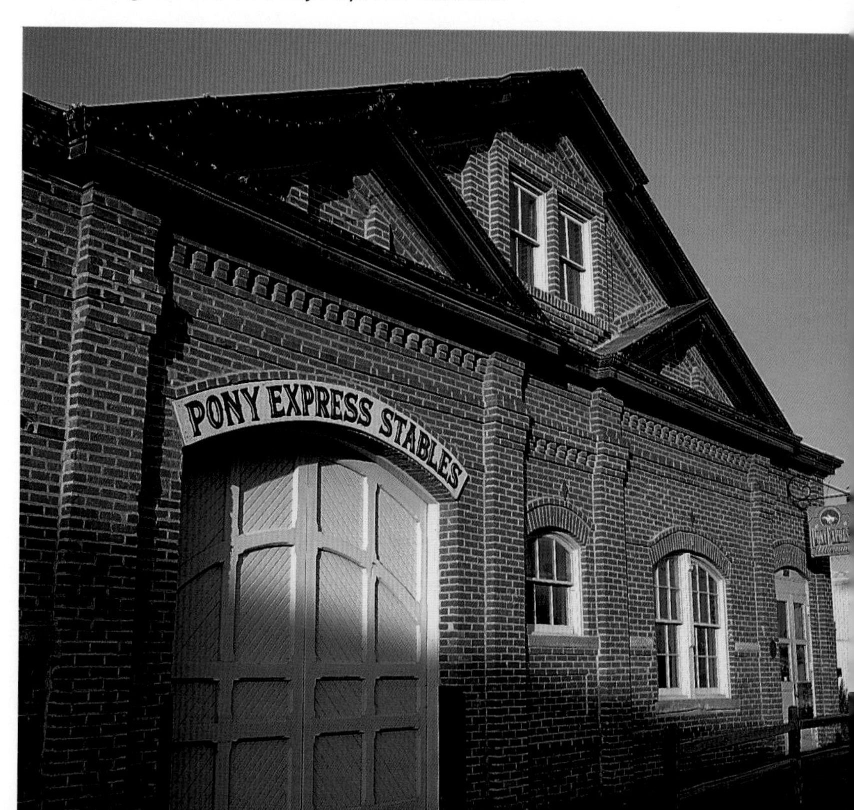

"Passing by Marysville, in old maps Palmetto City, a county town, which thrives by selling whisky to ruffians of all descriptions, we forded before sunset, the "Big Blue," a well-known tributary of the Kansas River. It is a pretty little stream, brisk and clear as crystal, about forty or fifty yards wide by 2-50 feet deep at the ford."

Sir Richard F. Burton, **The City of the Saints and Across the Rocky Mountains,** *1860.*

The route of the Pony Express stretched almost 2,000 miles across a wilderness. To manage such a far-flung enterprise, Russell, Majors, and Waddell divided the route into five separate divisions, numbered from east to west. There was one general superintendent, who had charge of the entire route, and a superintendent for each division. As can well be imagined, the division agent had a great deal of power on the lawless frontier—even to the power of life and death in some cases, although the company certainly would have disavowed that. "Home" stations were established anywhere from 65 to 100 miles apart, while "relay" or "swing" stations were about 25 miles apart at the onset of the Pony Express, although experience reduced this distance to 12 to 15 miles. The distance varied according to the difficulty of the terrain, with those in the wide-open plains farther apart than those in the mountains.

Home stations were usually those shared by the stagecoaches of the Overland Mail. They had a keeper, or agent, and five or six young helpers. In the more established home stations, the keeper's wife and children would also live there. The station keeper and his crew took care of the replacement horse herd, and provided bunks for the riders when they changed. They also provided fresh horses or mules, as well as meals and places to sleep for the tired, dusty passengers of the Overland Stage. Home stations in the eastern portion of the route were usually in a settled area, near a town or ranch. In the more remote corners of Utah and Nevada, a ranch was sometimes established where food could be grown. Besides corrals, barns, a home for the station keeper, and bunkhouses for the crew, there was always a blacksmith shop.

Relay stations were usually little more than tents, shacks, or dugouts, with one or two men, established near a source of (sometimes bad) water. The home stations were luxurious by comparison with the lonely relay stations, but life at both was typical of the frontier. Frigid in winter, boiling in summer, the stations were often in isolated areas, surrounded by forbidding deserts or endless plains and exposed to Indian attack. Excitement came once or twice a week, whenever a rider would suddenly appear in a cloud of dust; at the relay stations, he would leap from his horse, grab the *mochila*—the leather mailbag—and leap onto another horse. Then, in another flurry of dust and excitement, the rider would be off for the next leg of his journey. After the rider was on his way, life at the station would settle back into the tedium and routine so typical of frontier life.

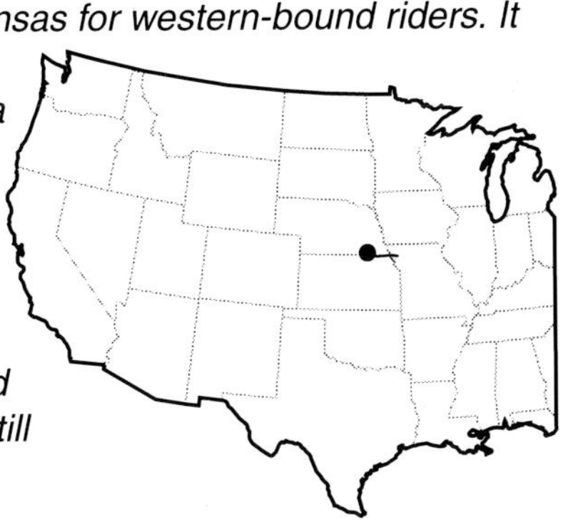

Hollenberg Station, also known as Cottonwood Station, was the last station in Kansas for western-bound riders. It also served travelers on the Oregon and California trails as a rest stop, where they could get food, livestock, and supplies. Today, Hollenberg Station is one of the few unchanged Pony Express buildings still on its original site.

Pony Express riders were glad to find ferries like this one over the Big Blue River at Marysville, Kansas. The town, originally named Palmetto City, was renamed Marysville after the wife of Frank Marshall, who operated the ferry. Riders stayed at the nearby American Hotel.

"One of the hardest rides I ever had made was when I carried President Lincoln's inaugural address from the telegraph station at Fort Kearney. Another was when the news came that Fort Sumter had been fired on. Such things broke the routine, and made every Pony Express rider feel that he was helping to make history."

William Campbell, 1932.

Division One of the Pony Express started at the Pony Express stables on Penn Street in St. Joseph, Missouri, on the banks of the Missouri River. The town had long been the traditional jumping-off place for explorers, fur trappers, freighters, and military expeditions to the lands of the western United States, so it was only natural that the Pony Express also made it their headquarters. The Patee House, currently listed on the National Register of Historic Places, housed the company offices. Coming or going, the riders would cross the Missouri on a steam ferry such as the little *Denver,* and be on their way. The first station in Kansas was at the little town of Troy. Legend has it that the Dooley girls of Troy would fry sweet dough and hand the pastries to Johnny Frye, one of the riders, as he galloped past. With his reins in one hand and a quirt in the other, he had a hard time grabbing the pastries, so the girls put a hole in the center of the pastry so Johnny could spear it with one finger as he passed; thus were donuts born.

From there to Fort Kearny, on the Platte River in Nebraska, there were 25 more stations. Since this part of the Pony Express route was through lands that had been settled for some time, the stations were generally more established and comfortable, with a home for the station keeper, an inn for passengers on the Overland, and facilities. Many of them were in small towns such as Troy, Atchison, and Marysville, while others were located near small but snug ranches. Most of the station keepers in Division One lived in reasonable comfort, such as Levi Hensel and his wife, who lived in a two-story house, held dances, and "set a splendid table." While settled, life was not always peaceful. On July 12, 1861, a gunfight erupted at Rock Creek Station in Nebraska between Wild Bill Hickok and David McCanles, the man who originally built the station. When it was over, three men lay dead, and Hickok and the station keeper were charged with murder. They were later acquitted.

The last station in Division One was at Fort Kearny, Nebraska, on the banks of the Platte River. By 1860, when the Pony Express riders began passing through, the troops from Fort Kearny had been protecting travelers on the Oregon and California trails for over ten years. A sod post office was opened at the fort in 1848, and Russell, Majors, and Waddell already used the fort as a station for their freight line, so it was a natural place to establish a Pony Express station. From there westward, the true frontier began—miles and miles of rolling plains; vast herds of buffalo; proud, unconquered tribes of Indians; and in the distance, a blue line on the horizon, the Rocky Mountains and the spine of the continent.

David McCanles bought the site of Rock Creek Station in 1859, and built a cabin and a toll bridge across the creek. The following year the Pony Express rented the cabin as a relay station and made McCanles the station keeper. Today, Rock Creek is a Nebraska state historical park.

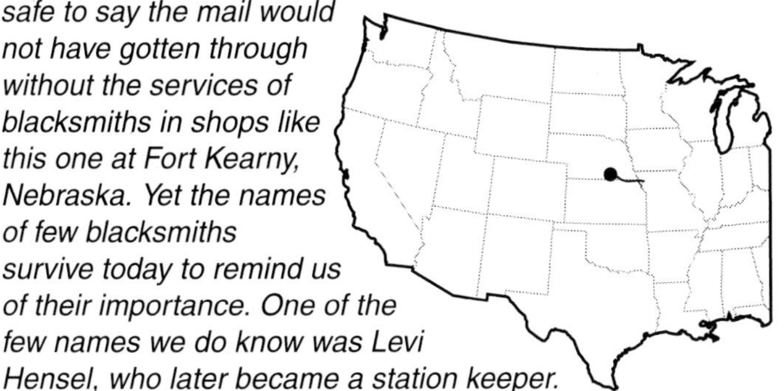

No occupation was more essential to an operation like the Pony Express than that of blacksmith. Traveling at high speed over rough terrain, horses often threw shoes, and it's safe to say the mail would not have gotten through without the services of blacksmiths in shops like this one at Fort Kearny, Nebraska. Yet the names of few blacksmiths survive today to remind us of their importance. One of the few names we do know was Levi Hensel, who later became a station keeper.

"The routes between St. Joseph, Missouri and Salt Lake City, and between Salt Lake and Placerville, California, have been so improved, that the trips through from St. Joseph to Placerville, and back, are performed once a week in thirty-eight days each way.... It has received from the people of California the warmest applause, and called forth public demonstrations of a most enthusiastic character."

U.S. Congress, Senate, Report of the Postmaster General, 1858.

Since the end of the Ice Age and the melting of the glaciers, vast herds of game and generations of Native Americans had followed the great rivers of the Plains back and forth across North America. In their turn, Spaniards, Frenchmen, American explorers, fur trappers, U.S. Cavalry, missionaries, and malcontents depended on the grass, water, and game found along the Missouri and the Platte rivers. So it was with the Oregon-bound families, the Mormons, and the Gold Rush Argonauts, and finally, with the riders of the Pony Express. Their route between Missouri and Salt Lake City varied in some small degree from the wagon road, since they could go places a heavy wagon couldn't, but for the most part they followed in the ruts of thousands who had preceded them.

The Oregon Trail was the first of these migration routes. Movement over it started as early as 1841. By the time of the Pony Express, less than two decades later, over half a million people had traveled the Oregon Trail at least as far west as Fort Bridger, in western Wyoming. Starting in 1847, over 70,000 Mormons followed the Oregon Trail to Fort Bridger, then picked up a barely visible track left by the Donner-Reed party of 1846. This they followed to their Promised Land in the Valley of the Great Salt Lake. And a scant two years later was the greatest migration of all—not for land, nor for religion, but for one of the most basic of human drives: wealth. The Gold Rush to California, beginning in 1849, brought tens of thousands of Argonauts, as they called themselves, creaking along the ruts of the Oregon and Mormon trails on their way to the goldfields. During one 18-month period, an official War Department report noted that more than 30,000 people had passed through Fort Kearny.

While emigrants and pony riders followed established roads to Salt Lake City, that was hardly the case to the west. The routes between Utah and California shared one characteristic: they were dangerous. Vast stretches of waterless desert, salt flats that concealed sucking mud, and high mountain passes, often choked with snow into the summer, meant that explorers and emigrants tried many different paths, often with tragic results. Still, through the efforts of Army explorers like John Charles Fremont, Capt. James Simpson, and "the lamented Gunnison"; Mormons like Oliver Huntington and George Washington Bean; and trail-blazing freighters like George Chorpenning and his agent Howard Egan, by the time the Pony Express riders galloped west from Salt Lake, a route had been laid out, and some stations established. While some of the mountain valleys along the route sheltered oases like Ruby Valley and Deep Creek, others were like Sand Springs, which Sir Richard Burton called a "vile hole" with water so alkaline that it would blister the hands. By the time the riders got to Carson City, Nevada, they were once again on long-established trails and, once over the Sierras, roads.

The Platte River was the great highroad to the west. Platte Station, a relay station for the Pony Express, was the first stop west of Fort Kearny. It was originally a stage stop for the Leavenworth and Pikes Peak Express Company.

Whether Machette's Station actually served as a Pony Express station remains controversial, but it occupied a site about 15 miles from where this log structure now stands. In 1931, the cabin was moved to Ehmen Park in Gothenburg, Nebraska, which now bills itself as "The Pony Express Capital of Nebraska." Today, the building houses a museum and a small gift shop, which sells Pony Express memorabilia.

"The station was sighted in a deep hollow. It had a good stone corral and the visual haystack, which fires on the hill seemed to menace.... The house was unusually neat, and displayed even signs of decoration in the adornment of the bunks with osier work taken from the neighboring creek."

Sir Richard F. Burton, **The City of the Saints and Across the Rocky Mountains,** *October 14, 1860.*

People all over the world recognize Buffalo Bill Cody, the most famous of the legendary pony riders. Many Americans might have heard of Billy Campbell, who lived the longest—or Broncho Charlie Miller, the youngest rider. But who's ever heard of Levi Hensel or David Lewis? How about David McCanles, killed in a gunfight with Wild Bill Hickok, or Howard Egan, a former bodyguard of the Mormon prophet Joseph Smith? All of the latter were station keepers on the Pony Express route. The riders, the popular heroes, could never have gotten through without them, but the only mark many of the keepers left on the West is their name on an obscure canyon. Many of their names are lost to history altogether.

Along the less-settled parts of the route, the station keepers lived in unbelievably harsh conditions and isolation, subject to storms, thirst, attacks by Indians, and loneliness. Sir Richard Burton, an Englishman who traveled the overland route during the time of the Pony Express, described the hard life of a station keeper: "...setting aside the chance of death...the work [is] severe; the diet is sometimes reduced to wolf-mutton, or a little boiled wheat and rye, and the drink to brackish water; a pound of tea comes occasionally, but the droughty souls are always out of whisky and tobacco."

It's easy to see how being a rider would attract young men, hungry for fame and adventure, but who was attracted to the lonely life of a relay station keeper in one of these remote outposts? The Pony Express naturally tried to use established ranches as much as possible; in some cases the rancher simply became the agent. But the fringes of the frontier always attracted men and some women who were marginalized by society, including the occasional desperado. In *Roughing It*, a book about his travels on the Overland Mail stagecoaches in 1860, Mark Twain wrote that a station keeper told him "there wasn't a man around there but had a price on his head and didn't dare show himself in the settlements." Since they were found in such isolation, stations were prime targets for Indians, and several were burned in Utah during the Pyramid Lake War in 1860. Some station keepers couldn't take it and moved on; not a few were killed. Despite the oath of sobriety that Majors forced them to swear when they signed on, many found less comfort in the leather-bound bible they were issued and more in the bottle, for few could withstand the months of toil, danger, and loneliness without an escape.

There is some doubt that William Frederick Cody, known to the world as Buffalo Bill, was a rider for the Pony Express when he was only 15 years old. The name "Buffalo Bill" comes from his service as a hunter of buffalo later in life. Scout's Rest Ranch, his home in North Platte, Nebraska, is now a Nebraska state historical park.

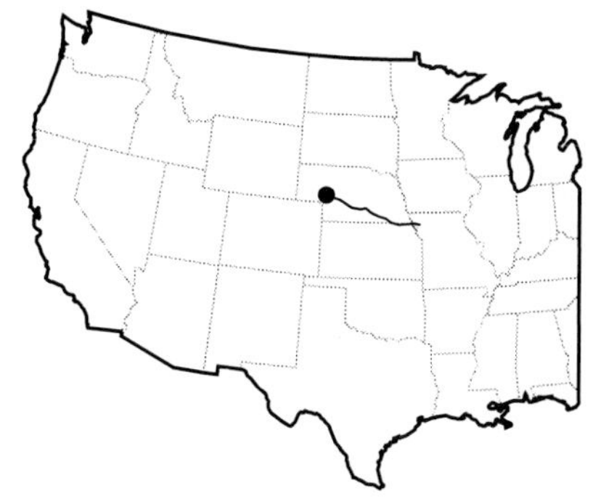

The lush rolling hills and springs in Cottonwood Canyon provided a reliable source of water—a natural place for a ranch and Pony Express station. Cottonwood Springs Station—also known as McDonald's Ranch—was also a stage stop.

"OVERLAND MAIL. MORE INDIAN TROUBLES. Springfield, MO., June 21.... The stations on the Pony Express line, and Salt Lake route, are known to have been destroyed, and the stock driven off over a distance of two hundred miles Eastward from Carson Valley. Parties of Indians constantly cross this route, and render it impossible to repair stations and restock the route unless United States troops are provided to protect it..."

Leavenworth **Daily Times**, *June 23, 1860.*

Things were going fine along the Pony Express route for the first month. Then in May 1860, trouble came, from a totally unexpected source. Since July 1859, miners had been pouring into the Washoe Hills of western Nevada. Gold and silver had been discovered there, and miners flocked by the thousands to the latest El Dorado. The Indians in the area lived a marginal existence anyway, and when they saw the influx of miners chasing off the scarce game, digging up the land, and building camps as if they intended to stay, the Indians began to grumble. When the Pony Express came, they built stations on water holes, critical to all life in these barren deserts. The winter of 1859-1860 was an especially harsh one, so in the spring of 1860, the Indians were convinced that the spirits of the land were telling them to do something about the white men.

The first hint of trouble came just a few weeks after the first ride, when Indians drove off the horse herd from the Roberts Creek station in western Nevada. A month later, Indians surrounded and burned the Williams station—with several men inside—to avenge an attack by the whites. The local miners formed a militia that finally defeated the Indians, but not before being ambushed on May 12, 1860, with dozens of miners killed and wounded.

So began a pattern of Indian raids in Nevada and Utah that cost the Pony Express dearly. It wasn't until June 25, 1860, that the first pony rider from the East reached San Francisco without delays en route. William Finney, company agent in San Francisco, raised his own troop of volunteers to travel the route eastward toward Salt Lake, rebuilding and reopening the stations. From Camp Floyd, in Utah, a troop of U.S. Cavalry started east with the same purpose. The fighting lasted sporadically throughout the summer.

Egan Canyon, July 16, 1860: the station keepers are surprised by 80 Shoshones demanding bread. The nervous men bake pan after pan of bread, and then watch in dismay as wood is piled around the station so it can be burned, with them in it. Just then, pounding hoofs announce the pony rider. He takes one look and wheels his lathered horse back around the way he'd just come, to alert a cavalry patrol a couple of miles back up the trail. Sixty troopers surround the station, and in the ensuing fight almost 20 Shoshones are killed. This is just one incident in a bitter little war that cost many men—both Indian and white—their lives, and the owners of the Pony Express $75,000, more than they could afford. It was a severe setback to the hopes of Russell, Majors, and Waddell, and yet another blow to the tribes of the Great Basin.

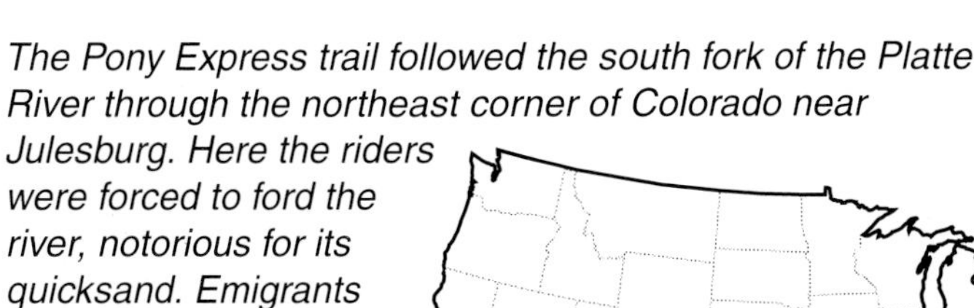

The Pony Express trail followed the south fork of the Platte River through the northeast corner of Colorado near Julesburg. Here the riders were forced to ford the river, notorious for its quicksand. Emigrants and stage drivers were often forced to "double-team" their horses or oxen to get the wagons safely across.

Many of the Pony Express stations across the Plains are marked by monuments such as this one at the site of Old Julesburg, near Ovid, Colorado. With a little planning and a good map, travelers can still follow the route of the Pony Express.

"The greatest danger I faced on the trail was buffaloes. They were along the trail in western Nebraska by thousands. If a rider even ran into a herd, he was gone. Wolves were numerous—big fellows. One winter night I saw some fifteen or twenty of them.... They followed me for fifteen miles to the next station."

William Campbell, 1932.

The stations from Fort Kearny westward were on the true frontier in 1860, and were not as well established as the ones in Kansas and eastern Nebraska. The route in Division Two followed the Oregon Trail, paralleling the Platte River before striking cross-country to the North Platte. From there it was all high plains and hard riding until the Horseshoe Creek station, just west of Fort Laramie. Along the way, if they'd had time to look at them, the pony riders passed two of the most famous landmarks of the Oregon Trail, Chimney Rock and Scotts Bluff, both visible for miles. Another famous landmark was Fort Laramie, by the time of the Pony Express already the best-known refuge along the Oregon Trail, or the "Great Medicine Road" as the Plains tribes called it. Hollywood films show a stockade, and one was planned, but Fort Laramie never had a wall around it.

The biggest problem in Division Two were the herds of buffalo that blocked the trail, and the packs of wolves that followed them. The riders were often shadowed by wolves, but fortunately they could find easier game than an armed rider on a fleet horse.

Riders changed horses in such remote spots as Cold Water Ranch Station, from whence Jim Moore made his famous emergency ride from Midway to Julesburg during the Indian troubles of June 1860; lonely Mud Springs, where Jim McArdle was the station keeper; and Julesburg, by 1860 a small town. It was originally a trading post founded by Jules Reni, who was hired as the station keeper for the Pony Express. Unfortunately, he didn't adhere to the oath given by Alexander Majors; company property and livestock began to disappear, wagon trains were attacked, and stage passengers robbed.

When the company learned that "Old Jules" himself was the leader of the outlaws, he was fired and replaced as division superintendent by Captain Jack Slade. Furious at being fired, Reni ambushed Slade with a shotgun and left him for dead, but amazingly, Slade survived—to Jules's regret, for when he recovered, Slade tracked Reni down, tied him to a corral post, and shot him full of holes. Slade then cut off his ears and carried them in his pocket as a souvenir. Slade was the most famous of the division superintendents. In *Roughing It*, Mark Twain called him a "high and efficient servant of the Overland, an outlaw among outlaws and yet their relentless scourge, Slade was at once the most bloody, the most dangerous, and the most valuable citizen that inhabited the savage fastnesses of the mountains." Slade later turned to crime himself, and was hanged by vigilantes in Montana.

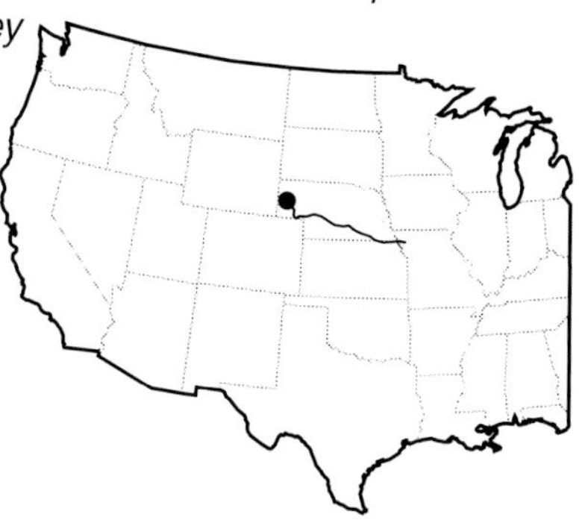

Chimney Rock, one of the most prominent landmarks on the Pony Express trail, stands 470 feet over the plains. Today, the nearby Chimney Rock Visitor Center documents the riders of the Pony Express, as well as travelers on the Oregon Trail.

When the Pony Express riders were crossing the Plains, bison still numbered in the millions, and the vast herds often blocked the trail. Within two decades, however, the bison had been decimated, and today small herds survive only in parks and wildlife reserves, and on private ranches.

"The mail must go. Hurled by flesh and blood across 2,000 miles of desolate space—Fort Kearney, Laramie, South Pass, Fort Bridger, Salt Lake City. Neither storms, fatigue, darkness, mountains and Indians, burning sands or snow must stop the precious bags. The mail must go."

Mayor M. Jeff Thompson, April 3, 1860.

William Russell boasted that the Pony Express would run on a weekly schedule, with each trip taking 240 hours, or ten days. The rider from St. Joseph left Friday mornings at 9:00 a.m., while the mail left San Francisco at 5:00 p.m. on Tuesdays. The Pony Express was expensive—to mail a letter cost $5.00 in gold per ounce or fraction thereof, quite a sum in those days when a dollar a day was considered good wages. Later, the use of special lightweight paper reduced the cost to $2.50, and still later it was reduced to $1.00 a half-ounce. The "Pony" also carried newspaper dispatches, likewise printed as special editions on lightweight paper. Indeed, the California press depended almost completely on the Pony Express. Western news was carried to St. Joseph, where it was telegraphed further east.

The mail was wrapped in oiled silk to protect it from rain and the sweaty horses, although that hardly worked when the horse was forced to swim a river. The first riders used a standard saddlebag, but later the company developed the *mochila*—Spanish for knapsack. About the size of a horse blanket, this was a single piece of leather with four pockets and a hole for the saddle horn. The *mochila* was thrown over the saddle and the rider sat on it, so it didn't need to be attached to the saddle and could be quickly changed. There were four *cantinas*, or pockets, at the corners; three of them were locked, with keys available only at army posts along the way, at the division headquarters in Salt Lake City, and at either end of the route. Each *mochila* carried from 12 to 15 pounds of mail. Some saddles and *mochilas* were made to company specifications, but many others were produced locally; most saddles were stripped down versions of the standard stock or army saddle.

The entire route covered over 1,900 miles, and it took about 75 horses to complete. The rider used three different changes of horses to make about 75 miles, although the distance varied according to weather and terrain. Once the *mochila* bearing the mails got to Sacramento or St. Joseph, the local newspaper would post an announcement of the arrival of the "Pony," with a list of names from the letters. On reading the announcement, people would come into the office to collect their mail.

At first the riders armed themselves with revolvers, bowie knives, and even carbines, but these proved too heavy and were soon discarded. At most the rider would carry a single revolver with extra cylinders; many went unarmed. It was company policy that they flee, not fight. They were never attacked by outlaws. Perhaps the outlaws knew that justice would be swift and harsh in those frontier times, when everyone was so dependent on the "Pony"; perhaps they shared a sense of the importance of linking the nation; most likely it was because they knew the Pony Express carried only mail, not gold or coin. Even without attacks by outlaws, Indians, or wolves, it was still hard work. Tom King, riding east from Salt Lake City to Ham's Fork in Wyoming, reported that he hadn't met the westbound rider, Henry Worley; Worley made the same report. But both made the journey safely—when they passed each other, they were sound asleep in the saddle.

The remains of Deer Creek Pony Express Station are located in the town of Glenrock, Wyoming. Deer Creek served as both a home and relay station and also boasted a post office and saloon.

Fort Laramie, in eastern Wyoming, was a major post during the era of travel on the Oregon, California, and Mormon trails, and had a Pony Express station as well. Today, Fort Laramie is a national historic site, with 11 rebuilt structures and living history programs.

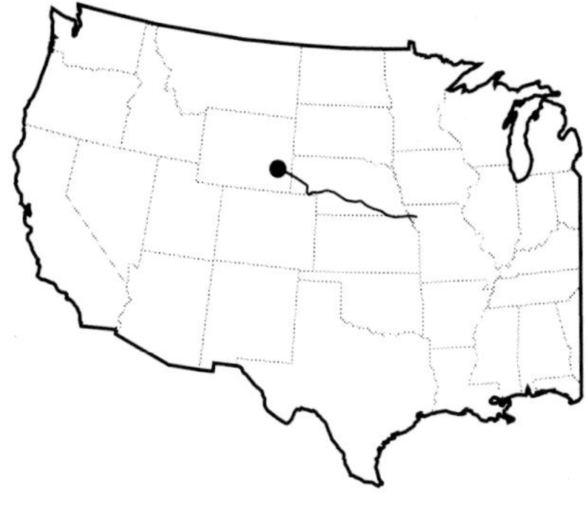

"The last express from the east...brought the result of the Chicago convention, by which it is made to appear that the Republicans have carried the war into Illinois by nominating Abraham Lincoln for President and Hannibal Hamblin of Maine for Vice President."

Salt Lake City **Deseret News**, *May 30, 1860.*

Division Three, from Horseshoe Creek, Wyoming, to Salt Lake City, was the second largest of the five. As the riders sped across the high desert of Wyoming, they crossed the backbone of the continent through South Pass, the gateway to the West for an entire generation of emigrants. In Division Three, the route finally left the Oregon Trail, which was well established before Salt Lake City was founded in 1847. The Oregon Trail and some routes of the California Trail veered to the northwest, toward Fort Hall, Idaho, while the Pony Express followed the Mormon and California trails through the rugged Wasatch Mountains to Great Salt Lake City, as it was still called, in the Valley of the Great Salt Lake.

After Horseshoe Creek came Elkhorn and La Bonte stations; next was charmingly-named Bed Tick Station, where the riders were no doubt glad that all they were doing was changing horses. The first significant station was Platte Bridge, located in present-day Casper, Wyoming. It was originally known as Mormon Ferry Post, after Mormon advance parties built and operated a ferry there in 1847. In 1859, Louis Guenot spanned the North Platte River with a 1,000-foot log bridge that reportedly cost $40,000. The Pony Express hired Guenot as station keeper and established Platte Bridge Station. Later renamed Fort Caspar, after a cavalryman who was killed in an Indian fight a few years later, it was one of the last and certainly the easiest crossing of North Platte River. From there was good going for the pony riders, except when rain turned the desert clay to deep mud. Today, this entire area is one vast oil and gas field, with wealth unimagined by the pony riders just beneath the pounding hooves of their horses.

From Platte Bridge the Sacramento-bound rider sped southwest, through Red Buttes, Willow Springs, Horse Creek, and Sweetwater stations. Devil's Gate Station, where the Sweetwater poured through a narrow opening, and Split Rock were more landmarks along the Oregon Trail. Nearby was Independence Rock, where travelers carved their names on the way west. The riders also passed close to Martin's Cove, where hundreds of snowbound Mormons, handcart pioneers, were trapped by early snowstorms and froze to death just a few years before. The Sweetwater River had to be forded at Three Crossings Station, while Ice Springs (where there was indeed ice in a subsurface cave almost all year round) was followed by Warm Springs Station. Climbing steadily, the rider was now near the fabled South Pass, that incongruous low, gentle crossing of the Rocky Mountains and the Continental Divide. South Pass was probably the most important geographic feature in the western United States, for wagons could easily be taken across the Continental Divide there. In later years, when the railroad was being built along this same route, South Pass City, a typical mining boomtown, would spring up at the site of South Pass Station. Today, near South Pass there is a pullout off the paved highway, with historic markers telling modern travelers about the Oregon Trail, the Overland Mail, and the Pony Express—but for the pony riders, it was just another place to change horses.

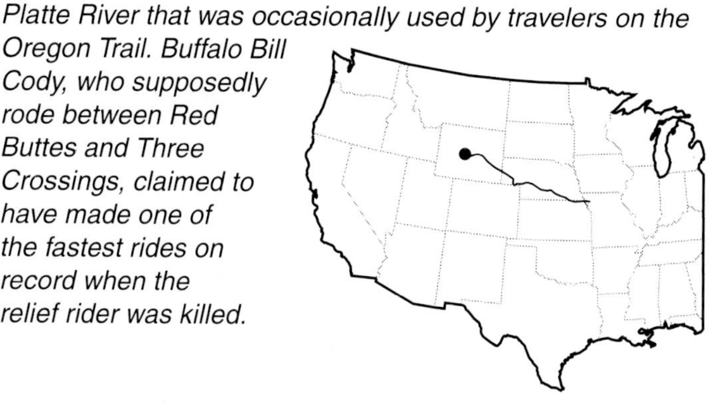

Red Buttes Station was located near a ford of the North Platte River that was occasionally used by travelers on the Oregon Trail. Buffalo Bill Cody, who supposedly rode between Red Buttes and Three Crossings, claimed to have made one of the fastest rides on record when the relief rider was killed.

Pony Express riders knew this site as Platte Bridge Station. It was renamed for Lt. Caspar Collins, who was killed by Indians while defending a wagon train on the Oregon Trail in July 1865. A frontier army clerk mistakenly changed the spelling to Casper.

"THE PONY EXPRESS. A marvel feat has been accomplished! The Pony Express has galloped across half the continent, and to-day the Pacific is in close neighborhood to the Atlantic. History will record this event as one of the gigantic private enterprises of our day."

Leavenworth **Daily Times**, *April 16, 1860.*

The three principals in the Central Overland California and Pikes Peak Express Company, or the Pony Express, were as different as three men could be. William Russell, the mastermind of the Pony Express, was the stereotypical western American entrepreneur. There was little middle ground among those who knew him—his friends called him a visionary and trusted him with their fortunes; his enemies, for enemies there were aplenty, called him improvident and reckless. By the outbreak of the Mexican War, he was a rich and successful freighter in Missouri; by the time he started the Pony Express, he was called the "Napoleon of the West."

Alexander Majors, the only true frontiersman among the three partners, grew up on the Missouri frontier. After trying his hand at farming, he started freighting in 1847, during the war with Mexico. Majors soon became one of the most trusted and successful freighters on the Santa Fe Trail, because his personality was the exact opposite of Russell's. He was steady and sober, and ran a very tight outfit; he had a wealth of first-hand trail experience and a hard-work ethic, never asking his employees to do something he wouldn't. He was the trail boss; he hired the drivers and riders, and required all employees to sign an oath of sobriety, loyalty, and general good behavior, a practice he carried on with the Pony Express. In many ways, the Pony Express, with its high risks and flashy image, was not to Majors's liking, but he was forced into it by his impulsive partner, William Russell.

William B. Waddell, the final partner, also found himself involved in the Pony Express because of his impetuous partner. Even though they were partners in the freighting business, no two men could be more dissimilar. Where Russell was extravagant with funds—usually other people's funds—Waddell was a cautious penny pincher; where Russell acted on impulse, Waddell only made decisions after ponderous deliberation. His association with Russell was the longest, having been a partner since the early 1840s.

In 1854, Russell, Majors, and Waddell formed a partnership to haul freight for the War Department, supplying posts west of the Missouri River. This gave them a virtual monopoly on freighting along the frontier. The three partners balanced each other out—Russell was the idea and public relations man, while the more conservative Majors and Waddell tended to tone down Russell's wildest flights of entrepreneurial fancy.

When gold was discovered in Colorado in 1858, Russell immediately started the Leavenworth and Pikes Peak Express Company without informing his partners. When this venture began to have problems, Russell characteristically—and again without the courtesy of letting his business partners know—started yet another company, the Central Overland California and Pikes Peak Express Company, known to history as the Pony Express.

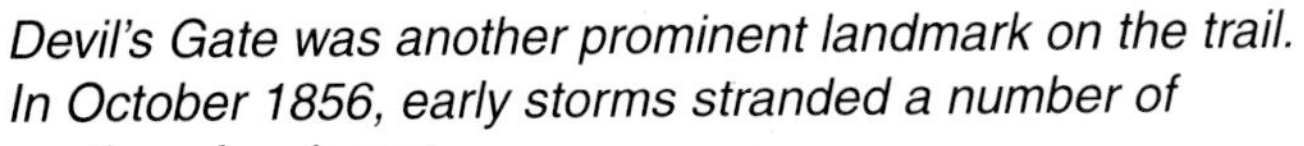

Devil's Gate was another prominent landmark on the trail. In October 1856, early storms stranded a number of parties of emigrant Mormons. The Martin company took refuge in a sheltered spot near Devil's Gate, since known as Martin's Cove, while they were waiting for rescuers from Salt Lake City.

Scenes like this beautiful field of lupines in the high desert of Wyoming must have often greeted the Pony Express riders, but they were too busy to notice or at least to record their thoughts.

"A person in the service of the Mail and Express company...reported that the weather had been very cold, and that the Indians...were in a destitute and starving condition. One Indian was recently found dead within a half mile of the station, who had perished of cold and starvation while on his way there for food.... Such a state of things among the red men is truly deplorable, but perhaps there is no way at present of ameliorating their condition."

Salt Lake City **Deseret News**, *February 20, 1861.*

From South Pass Station, it was downhill all the way to Salt Lake City. That's not to say the going got easier—far from it, for the western half of Division Three was the first place the Pony Express riders encountered significant mountains and canyons. They also began to encounter Mormons, for many members of that faith worked for the Pony Express, as riders, station keepers, and stock tenders. The first station after South Pass, Dry Sandy Station, was managed by a young Mormon couple, as were most of the others along this part of the route.

Not far past Dry Sandy Station (and Big Sandy and Little Sandy stations), came the first major river since leaving the Platte, the Green River. The Green is a major tributary of the Colorado, and though it was easy to ford in the summer, it was a raging torrent in the spring. During floods, the riders used the ferries that had been in place along the Green since 1847. Past the crossing was Michael Martin's Station, where the French-Canadian namesake of the station maintained a store, and Ham's Fork (named for mountain man Zacharia Ham), where David Lewis, a Scottish Mormon, kept the station together with his two polygamous wives.

Two more changes of horses brought the rider into Fort Bridger, second only to Fort Laramie in importance to travelers on the Oregon Trail. Mountain man Jim Bridger first explored the country north of the Uinta Mountains in the 1820s. In 1843, he and Louis Vasquez, another famous mountain man, built a trading post on the Black's Fork River. Within a few years, it was thriving. Travelers could get their wagons repaired, replace tired livestock, get trail directions from a mountain man, and purchase food, liquor, and ammunition at the fort. The Mormons took over the fort and the Green River ferries in 1854, and the U.S. Army—supplied by Russell, Majors, and Waddell—took it away from the Mormons during the Utah War of 1857-58. Judge W. A. Carter, who had a store and ran the post office, was also the station keeper at the fort.

West of Fort Bridger the route crossed into the Great Basin, that vast interior basin that makes up most of Utah and Nevada today. At Echo Canyon Station, the rider plunged into a deep canyon, following the rushing Weber River. A portion of Echo Canyon was the best route through the Wasatch Mountains, and the Mormons went that way in 1847. In 1858, Johnston's army of grumbling soldiers, fresh from a severe winter out on the plains west of Fort Bridger, marched down Echo Canyon, watched by Mormon guerrillas on the cliff tops. The railroad would later follow this natural route, and obliterate many landmarks along the way. At the mouth of Weber Canyon was Weber Station. Built in 1853, it boasted a stone stage station, an inn, a general store, and a saloon. The station keeper "maintained a large supply of food for man and beast in the form of locally grown vegetables and wild hay." East Canyon Station, a bit further on, was managed by Ephraim Hanks, a member of the notorious Danites, or Mormon Militia. Next stop: Salt Lake City!

Travelers on the Oregon Trail often took alternate routes like the Seminoe Cutoff to avoid paying tolls at a river crossing or, in this case, crossing a rocky ridge. The Warm Springs Pony Express station, one of many on the high desert of Wyoming, was nearby.

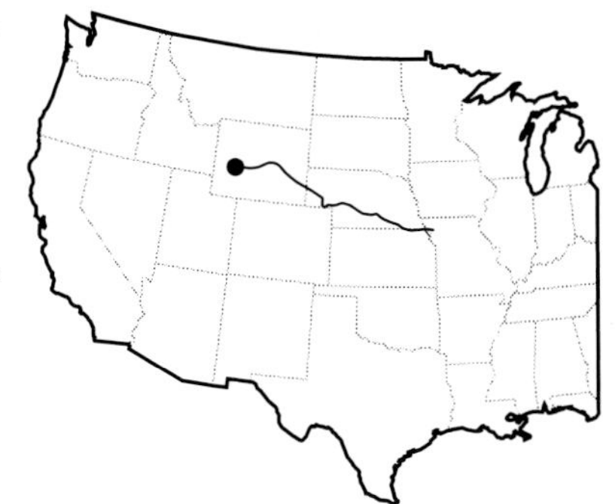

Prairie dog burrows were a real hazard to Pony Express riders, since a horse could stumble in the hole and throw the rider. Vast prairie dog "towns" were once found in the Great Plains from Canada to Mexico, but today their numbers have been reduced to the point that prairie dogs are listed as an endangered species.

*"**HERE HE COMES!** Every neck is stretched further, and every eye strained wider. Away across the endless dead level of the prairie a black speck appears against the sky, and it is plain that it moves. Well, I should think so! In a second or two it becomes a horse and rider, rising and falling, rising and falling—sweeping toward us nearer and nearer—growing more and more distinct, more and more sharply defined—nearer and still nearer, and the flutter of the hoofs comes faintly to the ear—another instant, a whoop and hurrah from our upper deck, a wave of the rider's hand, but not reply, and man and horse burst past our excited faces, and go winging away like a belated fragment of a storm!"*

Mark Twain, **Roughing It**, *1872.*

Few images in American history have more romance than the galloping Pony Express rider on his lathered steed, fighting off Indian attacks or outdistancing howling wolves, no doubt saying to himself through clenched teeth "The mail must go through!" While there's a great deal of truth in that image, like so much romance there's also a lot of wishful thinking. There were never more than 80 or so riders, although hundreds later claimed the honor. It wasn't for lack of applicants—when the division agent in Sacramento advertised that he needed 50 riders, over 200 hopefuls showed up.

Naturally, small, lightweight men were preferred, but the apocryphal newspaper advertisement calling for young, wiry, expert horsemen, preferably orphans, hides the fact that the riders came from all walks of life and were all ages. There were native-born Americans, French, German, and Italian emigrants, and at least one Mexican-American who was killed in the Pyramid Lake War. The youngest was reputedly only 13 years old, although like so many things about the Pony Express, there is considerable doubt as to the veracity of the claim.

Each man was given a calf-bound bible, and had to swear the oath of the Pony Express. This oath was probably easier for the riders than the station keepers to hold to, since they were always on the move. The riders were at first paid only $50 a month, although this was later raised, and those who had to make longer rides during an emergency sometimes got bonuses. When William Russell's financial house of cards started to fall apart, the riders suffered. Wags among them started calling it the "Clean Out of Cash and Poor Pay Express Company."

They earned every cent of their pay, for it was hard, dangerous work. Accidents were common, and several riders were killed in falls. At least one simply disappeared; his riderless horse came into the station east of Carson City in August 1860, and he was never found. In December 1860, a rider unfamiliar with the route froze to death near Fort Kearny. But there was never a shortage of riders. They were young and cocky, and they all knew they were making history as they rode. Theirs was a tight bond, too—Richard Erastus Egan, son of Division Four superintendent Howard Egan, once rode 330 miles, twice the normal distance, to allow one of his comrades to visit a sweetheart.

There was once a Pony Express station right at the summit of historic South Pass; today, little remains save ruts stretching off into the distance. All early travelers celebrated at nearby Pacific Springs, since they had now crossed the Continental Divide.

This stone is near where the Pony Express route left the Oregon Trail for the last time, to follow the Mormon Trail. The Oregon Trail veered northwest toward Fort Hall, Idaho, while the Mormon Trail continued southwest to the Wasatch Mountains and Salt Lake City.

ICE HOUSE

"At 6:30 P.M., we debouched upon the bank of the Green River.... The station had the indescribable scent of a Hindoo village, which appears to result from the burning of **bois de vache** *and the presence of cattle: there were sheep, horses, mules, and a few cows, the latter so lively that it was impossible to milk them.... We supped comfortably at Green-River Station, they supplying excellent salmon trout. The kichimichi, or buffalo berry, makes tolerable jelly, and alongside the station is a store where Mr. Burton (of Maine) sells 'Valley Tan' whisky."*

Sir Richard F. Burton, **The City of the Saints and Across the Rocky Mountains,** *1860.*

When Russell, Majors, and Waddell announced the creation of the Pony Express on January 27, 1860, they had only 60 days to organize their venture. There was so much to do that they must have wondered what to do first. Since Russell, Majors, and Waddell was already hauling freight over the Oregon and Mormon trails to Salt Lake City, selecting the route—at least that leg of it—was easy. Next, they had to decide on an eastern and a western terminus of the route. Sacramento was never in doubt as the western end, and the city fathers of Lexington, Missouri, where Russell, Majors, and Waddell was already based, were sure the honor of the eastern terminus would fall to them. But to their surprise and dismay, St. Joseph, Missouri, won the nod. The railroad and the telegraph ended there; it was the largest town on the Missouri River; and the town fathers were willing to make concessions, such as donating land, offices, and corrals. St. Joe it was.

Next they had to quickly establish central offices at the ends of the route, hire company agents in New York, Washington, Chicago, St. Louis, Denver, Salt Lake, and San Francisco, and hire a general superintendent and division superintendents. Benjamin Ficklin, already in their employ, was made the general superintendent, with responsibility for the whole route. A. E. Lewis was hired for Division One, from St. Joseph, Missouri, to Fort Kearny. Division Two, stretching across the Great Plains from Fort Kearny to Horseshoe Station, near Fort Laramie, Wyoming, needed a strong hand—the famous Joseph "Jack" Slade. Division Three went from Horseshoe Station to Salt Lake City; James Bromley became superintendent.

Now they had to hire 80 riders and about 200 other personnel, and establish home and relay stations all the way from St. Joe to Salt Lake City. Fortunately, the home stations could be shared with the Overland Mail, and the relay stations could be set up at the many ranches along the route. To save time and money, the partners often simply hired a rancher, if he was in the right spot, although this sometimes had disastrous consequences, such as the case of Jules Reni, a notorious outlaw. Some of the difficulties were political—tying down the mail contracts from the government, and getting the support of the right congressmen for future contracts. For this William Russell was ideally suited.

When all this was done, it must have been a great relief. Surely running the mails couldn't be as hard as setting it all up?

In August 1860, Sir Richard Burton was delighted to find "no less than three Englishwomen" living at Green River Station near Castle Rock. The company, and a visit to the local "grog-shop," enabled Burton to "pass a comfortable night in the store."

Few places were as important to early travelers as Fort Bridger, Wyoming, where the Pony Express maintained a station. The fort was an oasis of civilization and plenty along a route that crossed an empty wilderness. Today, visitors can wander among restored and historic buildings, and enjoy interpretive programs at the fort.

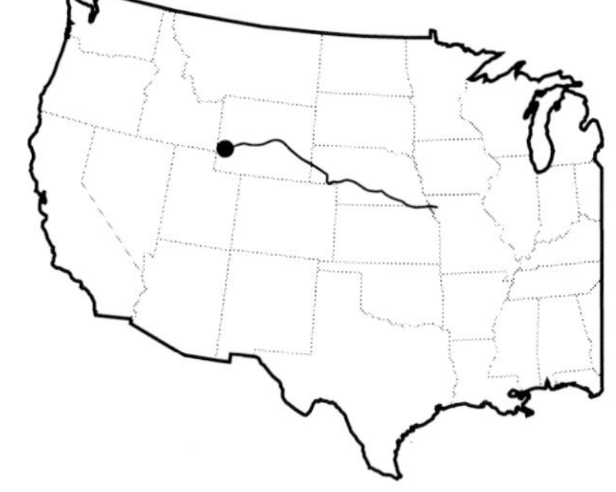

Overleaf: Split Rock in Wyoming's Granite Mountains.

"We had orders on that first run to do our level best.... My run on that record-breaking ride was fifty-seven miles. We did not have the stations then to change horses. I had to make it with just one horse and I made the run in mighty good time considering the distance, but I killed the poor horse in doing it."

George Washington Perkins.

Like their riders, the horses used by the Pony Express came from local sources. On the eastern end of the line, William Russell advertised in the local newspapers for 200 gray mares, four to seven years old, about 15 hands high (mid-size for a horse). Riders on the Plains used former U.S. Cavalry mounts. In Utah, wild horses were rounded up by local Mormons, broken for riding, and sold to the Pony Express. William Finney bought half-breed California mustangs, "alert and energetic as their riders." The Pony Express needed horses that could handle the local conditions. In the West, they wanted small, tough, sure-footed mountain ponies that could work in the Sierra Nevada and the endless, lonely mountain ranges of central Nevada. Out on the Great Plains, the horses could be bigger and faster. They almost always bought mares—stallions might have greater speed, but they needed the reliability and steady strength of the mare.

The Pony Express bought some 400 to 500 horses, sometimes for as much as $200 per head, a high price for the times. The total cost was around $87,000, an indication that they valued horseflesh at least as much as, if not more than, they valued the riders. The mounts were supposed to be at least partially broken to the saddle, although Levi Hensel, a blacksmith and later station keeper in Kansas, called some of the horses in his area "imps of Satan."

The company then had to gather the horses at central locations like Camp Floyd, Utah, where the Pony Express maintained a huge horse herd in nearby Rush Valley. Each horse was expected to be good for about 25 miles, although there were numerous instances of horses and riders being forced by Indian attack or weather to go two and even three times that distance. Like their riders, many horses were casualties of the pressure to get the mail through; tales abound of riders being thrown by the horse stumbling, with little record of what became of the horse. Some were ridden literally to death. A bay mare used on the first ride suffered a different kind of trouble—souvenir hunters in St. Joseph, waiting for the ride to begin, plucked so many hairs from her tail to make into watch chains and rings that the poor horse became frantic and had to be put back in her stall until it was time to go. Many horses were stolen by the Shoshones and Goshutes during the Indian troubles in the summer of 1860, and their feral descendants still roam the wild wastes of western Utah and eastern Nevada to this day.

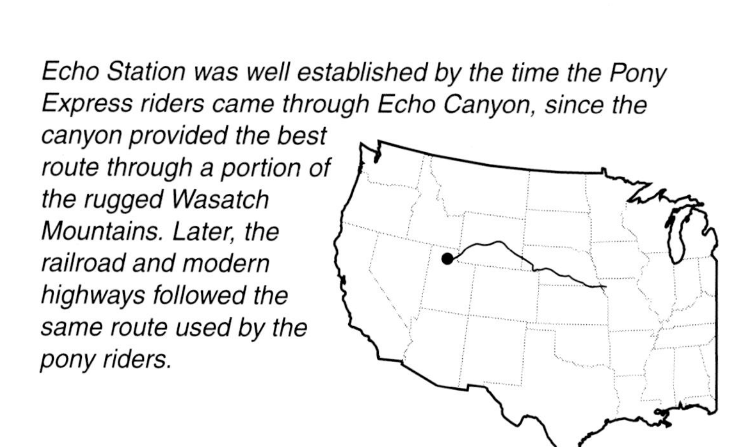

Echo Station was well established by the time the Pony Express riders came through Echo Canyon, since the canyon provided the best route through a portion of the rugged Wasatch Mountains. Later, the railroad and modern highways followed the same route used by the pony riders.

This Is the Place Monument stands at This Is the Place Heritage Park in Salt Lake City, an open-air museum honoring Utah pioneers. A new statue—one of two by noted Utah sculptor Award Fairbanks—adjacent to this monument honors the Pony Express. Its dedication in July 1998 drew over 10,000 people.

"There were about eighty pony riders in the saddle all the time, night and day, stretching in a long, scattering procession from Missouri to California, forty flying eastward, and forty toward the west, and among them making four hundred gallant horses earn a stirring livelihood and see a deal of scenery every single day of the year."

Mark Twain, **Roughing It**, *1872.*

If setting up the Pony Express from St. Joseph to Salt Lake City was difficult, organizing the line from Salt Lake City westward must have seemed almost impossible. Howard Egan, who had gotten his start with Chorpenning's stage line, was the superintendent of Division Four, which stretched from Salt Lake City to Roberts Creek, Nevada. From Roberts Creek (named for the division superintendent, Bolivar Roberts) to Sacramento was Division Five, the largest of the divisions. From Sacramento, the mail was carried on the American River by steamboat to San Francisco, although on quite a few occasions the mail had to go all the way to San Francisco by Pony Express.

True, there were a few stations already established by George Chorpenning, but since he ran his own passenger line along the same route until May 1860 and wasn't willing to share his stations, the Pony Express had to build most of theirs from scratch. Wagon trains were sent out from Salt Lake City and Sacramento laden with supplies and building materials, with crews to construct the needed home and relay stations. Some were natural oases like Ruby Valley and Deep Creek, where the Pony Express soon established productive farms and ranches. But others, like Sand Springs, where the water was so bad it was ringed with the skeletons of animals that had died after drinking it; and Dugway Station, on the edge of the dreaded Forty Mile Desert, could at best be described as hardship duty. They were not placed there for comfort or convenience, but simply because it was as far as a horse could go without injury (not that they were especially solicitous of the horses, but a lame horse couldn't carry the mail).

At the worst of them, everything—brooms, candles, well wheels, buckets, rope, doors, dishes, horse brushes, wagon grease, food, hay, grain, illicit liquor, ammunition, even water—had to be hauled in by wagon, and it was hard to find men willing to live in such conditions. The stations in Utah and Nevada were the most exposed to Indian attack, and suffered greatly during the Pyramid Lake War. There were other hardships, such as building the "corduroy" roads through the Humboldt Sink, when the men were covered with clouds of mosquitoes. But once the line reached Carson City, civilization reappeared, and although the route over the Sierras was difficult and could be dangerous, at least it was well established. It was with good reason that the western half of the route was known as the "Siberia of the Pony Express."

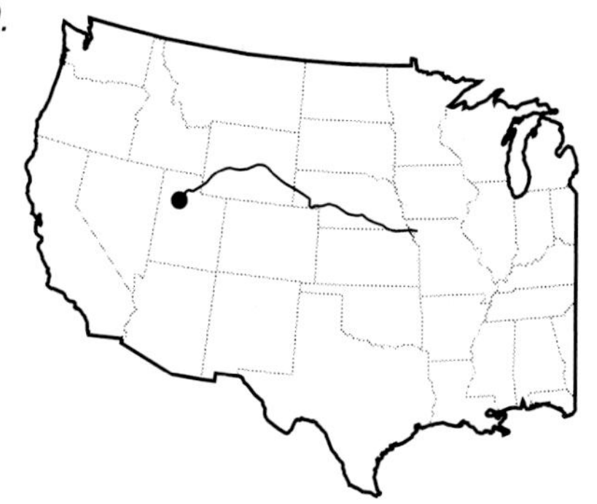

Simpson Springs is named for army explorer James H. Simpson, who laid out a route between Salt Lake City and Carson City in 1859. The rock Pony Express station was rebuilt by the Bureau of Land Management in 1975. Today's visitors can enjoy interpretive signs that recount the station's history.

One of the compensations for station keepers in the lonely stretches of the Pony Express route in western Utah must have been beautiful sunsets such as this one over Simpson Butte. The riders had little time to enjoy sunsets, though—they had a schedule to keep!

"At 4 P.M. we reached the settlement consisting of two huts and a station-house, a large and respectable-looking building of unburnt brick, surrounded by fenced fields, water-courses, and stacks of good adobe.... The station was dirty to the last degree: the flies suggested the Egyptian plague; they could be brushed from the walls in thousands; but, though sage makes good brooms, no one cares to sweep clean."

Sir Richard F. Burton, **The City of the Saints and Across the Rocky Mountains,** *1860.*

Salt Lake City and Camp Floyd, Utah, were the two most important Pony Express stations in Division Four. The two places were mirror images of each other: one the Promised Land, the City of the Saints, ruled by an unquestioned theocracy; the other typical of the boomtowns that surrounded frontier army posts, "a riffraff of saloon-keepers, gamblers, women, slickers, thieves, and robbers."

Since Salt Lake City was the only settlement of any size for most of the route, it was naturally an important Pony Express station. The company offices were in the Salt Lake House, at 143 South Main Street. Sir Richard Burton said that he "had not seen aught so grand for many a day," but noted that many rough-looking characters hung around the offices.

Two blocks up Main Street was Brigham Young's office. Young—the "Prophet, Seer, and Revelator" of the Mormon faith—often thundered from the pulpit about being self-sufficient, but secretly welcomed the news and business that the Pony Express brought. The Mormons planned to establish a pony express of their own, but the Utah War of 1857-58 intervened, and the proposed service never got started. With President Young's approval, when the "Pony" arrived from back east, the Mormon newspaper, the *Deseret News*, published an extra called the *PONY DISPATCH.* Also with his approval—for little occurred in Utah without it—many Mormons worked for the Pony Express as riders, agents, station keepers, and stock tenders. Food and hay grown by Mormon farmers fed the riders and the horses, which were purchased from Mormons.

Camp Floyd was a result of compromises between Brigham Young and the United States that averted bloodshed in the Utah War. After marching through Salt Lake City to a valley about 40 miles southwest, the troops established a post named after John Floyd, Secretary of War. For much of its brief existence, it was the largest army post in the country. Again, it was only natural that it became an important Pony Express station, although John Carson, the station keeper, was a good Mormon who didn't allow "riffraff" on the premises. This "oasis of decency" was the Fairfield House, a two-story adobe inn that had been built in 1858.

Camp Floyd Station served as a jumping-off place for riders headed out into the desert wastes to the west. There were extensive hay fields and gardens there, and the Pony Express kept huge herds of replacement horses in the lush valleys near Camp Floyd. When the Pony Express brought news of the outbreak of the Civil War, the soldiers also learned that John Floyd had defected to the south, so the post was renamed Camp Crittenden. Soon, the troops were called east to fight, and the post was abandoned. Only the Fairfield House, now a Utah state park, still stands as a monument to the Pony Express.

Boyd's Station, near the Nevada border, is one of the few remaining Pony Express stations in Utah. The Bureau of Land Management maintains the site, and has provided interpretive signs as well as conducting stabilization of the ruins. Bid Boyd, the station keeper, reportedly lived on at the site into the twentieth century.

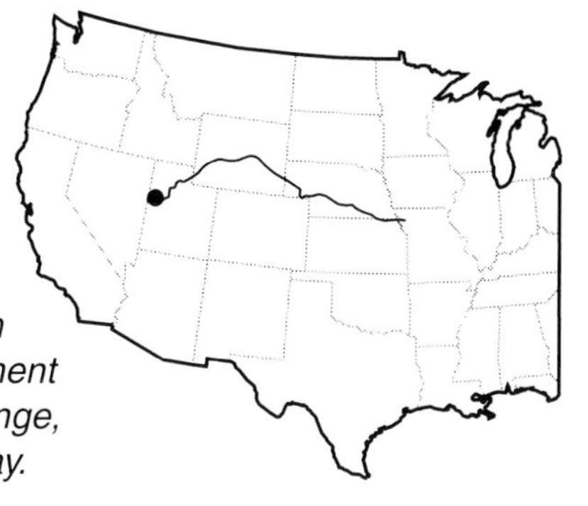

The Great Salt Lake Desert is some of the most inhospitable country in the United States. Much of the land in western Utah traversed by the Pony Express riders was taken over by the U.S. government in 1940 for a bombing range, and remains so to this day.

"...we had to build willow roads, corduroy fashion, across many of the places along the Carson River, carrying bundles of willows two or three hundred yards in our arms. The mosquitoes were so thick that it was difficult to tell whether the man was white or black, so thickly were they piled on the neck, face and arms."

Jay G. Kelley.

West from Camp Floyd the riders were entering a vast wasteland of mudflats, lonely mountain passes, and hostile tribes. But the mail had to go through, even if it meant crossing what is still some of the most remote and unpopulated land in the United States. Not all of it was howling wilderness—there were places with good water and soil like Ruby Valley, Deep Creek, and Simpson Springs. Deep Creek in western Utah was the home station of Howard Egan, superintendent of Division Four. Richard Burton described the station as "two huts and a station-house, a large and respectable-looking building of unburnt brick, surrounded by fenced fields, water-courses, and stacks of good adobe." Likewise, Ruby Valley Station in Nevada was a true oasis in the middle of the Great Basin desert. Originally one of Chorpenning's stations, the Pony Express improved it with new buildings, and raised food for horses and men.

But most of the stations in western Utah and eastern Nevada were little better than hovels. Horace Greeley called Dugway "about the forlornest spot I ever saw," while Burton went further, saying it was "...a mere 'dugout'—a hole four feet deep, roofed over with split cedar trunks, and provided with a rude adobe chimney." Three wells were dug near the station, and one reached a depth of 150 feet, but nothing wet was ever found and water had to be hauled from Riverbed or Simpson's Springs. Butte Station in Nevada had its own spring enclosed within an adobe wall, but had no windows, just rifle ports. It was called Robber's Roost or Thieves' Delight by other Pony Express employees—the men at this isolated post generally valued the distance from civilization. Water was so scarce that riders were only offered a handful of gravel to remove the dust of travel. Burton noted that at some stations "the flies suggested the Egyptian plague."

Division Four was beset by Indian troubles from the very beginning. Schell Station, Egan Canyon, even Butte Station, despite its strong defenses, were burned in 1860. The employees at these lonely stations lived in constant fear, and were frequently forced to "fort up" to escape roving bands of warriors. There were exceptions—Fred Hurst, the Mormon station keeper at Ruby Valley, was friendly with the local bands and was often warned when war parties were approaching. Even with bad water and Indians, the worst enemy of the men who worked for the Pony Express was often boredom. Richard Burton describes how a station master in Nevada "...amused himself by decorating the sides of the [dugout] with niches and Egyptian heads." Finally, as if loneliness, bad water, and danger weren't enough, the Overland Mail reported that the reason they couldn't keep help at the nearby Riverbed Station was because it was haunted by "desert fairies."

Travel through the wild stretches of Utah and Nevada was often dangerous, but in good weather it was much like crossing the Great Plains. On the flat playas, *or dry lake beds, and through the low mountain ranges, the riders could often make good time.*

Much of the Pony Express route through Utah and Nevada can still be followed today. The trails were later improved by ranchers and the government, and a number of guidebooks are available at bookstores. It's still wild, uninhabited country, though, and anyone planning to travel the route should be well prepared.

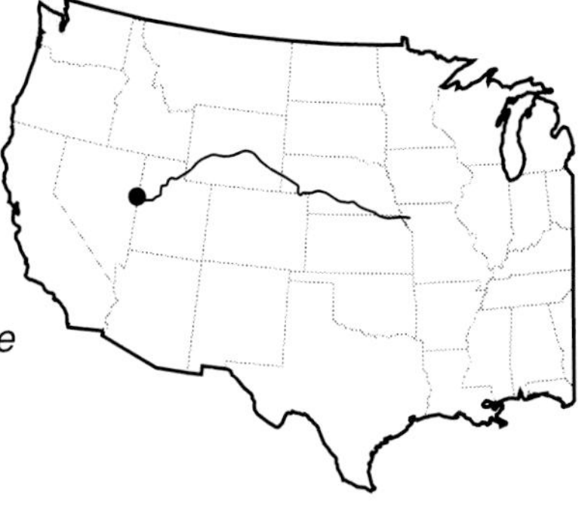

"It was not until December, 1860, that I had an opportunity to ride. The boys were dropping out pretty fast. Some of them could not stand the strain of the constant riding. It was not so bad in summer, but when winter came on, the job was too much for them.... My first ride was in a heavy snow storm, and it pretty nearly used me up."

William Campbell, 1932.

Even as the Pony Express riders were traversing the continent to the acclaim of the world, and the envy of the boys and admiration of the girls in all the towns they passed, the seeds of its end were already sprouting. In June 1861, Overland Telegraph Company crews planted their first pole east of Fort Churchill, Nevada. Constructing a new telegraph station every 50 miles, the company hoped to string 5 miles of wire a day. The telegraph crews followed the same route as the Pony Express and Overland Mail, so each 50 miles of wire cut off five hours of riding. The telegraph started west from St. Joseph to Fort Kearny in 1860. In the same manner as the railroad was built a few years later, crews from east and west built toward each other, planning to meet in Salt Lake City. It was an exciting time—the nation held its collective breath as each new express from the "Pony" brought news of the progress of the telegraph. By July 26, 1861, the line reached isolated Sand Springs Station in Nevada; by August 8 it was at Reese River Station, a hundred miles further east. That same month, the west-building crews were 50 miles west of Fort Kearny. When a crew from Salt Lake City started building eastwards, everyone knew it couldn't be long.

Interestingly, usage of the Pony Express actually went up as the telegraph lines neared completion, because the public wanted faster and faster service. The secession crisis was the worst the country had ever faced, and people in the West wanted to know each new development as soon as they could. The pony riders carried telegrams between the ends of the wires, but still carried letters, newspapers, and other mail the entire distance right up until the end. There was a great rivalry between the telegraph crews, and the line was finished October 24, 1861, with the first westbound wire arriving on October 20 and the first eastbound wire arriving on October 24. On October 26, the first news dispatch was sent coast to coast. The last Pony Express package was delivered in November, since everything in transit had to be delivered.

Amazingly, even with virtually instant communications now available, many in California still felt there was a need for the Pony Express. The telegraph suffered many teething troubles, and the service was not always reliable. Buffalo would lean against the posts and knock them over, or Indians, who sensed the significance of the "talking wires," would throw a rope over the wire and drag down miles of it. Even the Overland Mail drivers were sometimes guilty of stealing wire to repair their coaches. The San Francisco *Evening Bulletin* stated in an editorial that "We need a well organized Pony Express, to...make our communication with the Atlantic States as perfect as it can be."

But it was all to no avail. A bill passed by Congress authorizing the Overland Telegraph included a provision that the Pony Express would be discontinued as soon as the telegraph was completed. The fate of the Pony Express was sealed by the humming of the wires.

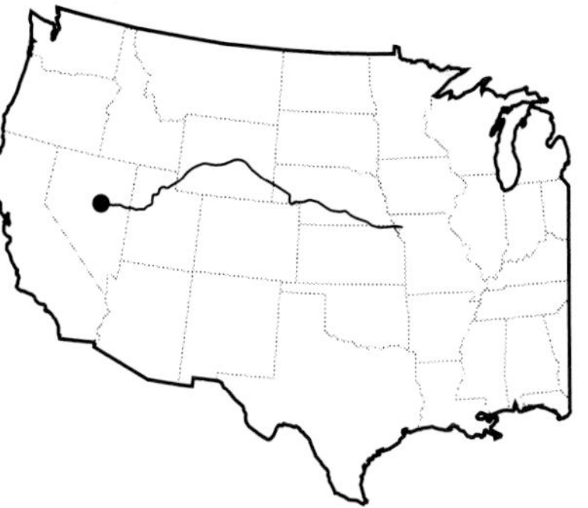

Along the more established sections of the Pony Express route, riders could often get through by following mule-train and stagecoach traffic. In the isolated Great Basin, however, there was no one to break trail when heavy snow blanketed the ground, and the Pony Express ground to a halt.

The telegraph followed the Pony Express across the plains, mountains, and deserts. Many of the Pony Express stations were later used by the telegraph operators. Although the wires were long since taken down for scrap, in some places glass insulators can still be found, and the stumps of telegraph poles can still be seen.

"The station is named Diamond Springs, from an eye of warm, but sweet and beautifully clear water bubbling up from the earth. A little below it drains off in a deep rushy ditch, with a gravel bottom, containing equal parts of comminuted shells: we found it an agreeable and opportune bath."

Sir Richard F. Burton, **The City of the Saints and Across the Rocky Mountains,** *1860.*

Division Five, which covered western Nevada and California, contained the most stations of any division of the Pony Express. There was a great disparity in conditions endured by the riders and station keepers. Working in western Nevada could be an ordeal of bad water, loneliness, harsh weather, and danger from Indians, while from Carson City, Nevada, to the end of the line in San Francisco, the route passed through settled towns and villages. Except for snowstorms in the Sierra Nevada, life at those stations was fairly comfortable.

The worst of the stations in Division Five, and one of the worst on the entire Pony Express route, was Sand Springs in Nevada. It was built on the only water for miles, but the water was "warm, smelly, and had a taste equal to rinsing a mail rider's socks." A pioneer of 1861 said the station was a pole stuck in the sand, covered by a scrap of canvas, "no fence, not even a stone or stick for fuel." There wasn't even any grazing for the horses; everything had to be brought in by wagon.

Other stations weren't quite so bad. Simpson Park, in about the middle of Nevada, had abundant wood, water, and grass. Bucklands Station, named for the station keeper, Samuel S. Buckland, a former Argonaut, had been built in 1859 and had a ranch, a hotel, and a bridge over the Carson River. In 1859, when the mail route was shifted south from the old emigrant trail along the Humboldt River to the central overland route, George Chorpenning built the Carson Sink station. It had a good spring, and boasted frame buildings surrounded by an adobe wall, which doubled as a corral and fort. Mosquitoes were a problem during the warmer months, but at least the water was drinkable.

One thing all of the stations in western Nevada shared was danger from Indian attack. It was an incident at Williams Station that sparked the Pyramid Lake War in 1860. During the entire existence of the Pony Express, none of the stations in Nevada and Utah were safe from attack. When Sir Richard Burton passed through on the Overland Mail coach in October 1860, he found many of the stations just then being rebuilt after being burned by Indians. Virtually every station between Salt Lake City and Carson City was attacked at one time or another during the time the Pony Express was operating.

It was to combat the Indians that Captain Joseph Stewart and his men built an adobe fort about 25 miles from Comstock, Nevada, in July 1860, and named it Fort Churchill. When Bucklands Station was attacked once too often by Indians, the Pony Express moved its station to the fort. It was one of the few places on the entire route about which Sir Richard Burton had something good to say.

According to Sir Richard Burton, Diamond Springs Station was named for the "warm, but sweet and beautifully clear water bubbling up from the earth." The refreshing water was in stark contrast to the next station down the line, Sulphur Springs. Today, the springs still flow, and a monument stands about a mile from the site of the station.

NEVADA HISTORICAL SOCIETY

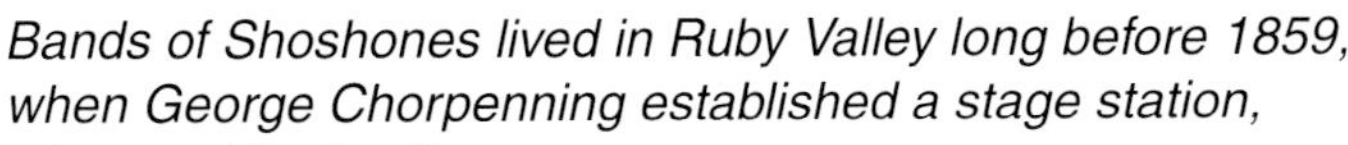

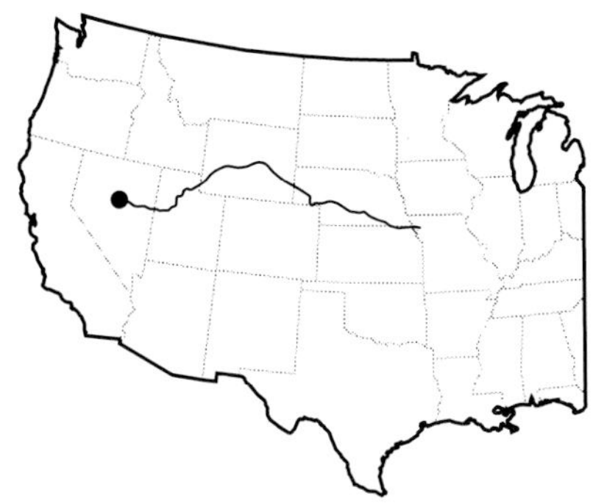

Bands of Shoshones lived in Ruby Valley long before 1859, when George Chorpenning established a stage station, later used by the Pony Express and the Overland Mail. During the Pyramid Lake Indian War, Company B of the 4th Artillery Regiment was stationed there to protect the route.

"The Express encountered serious obstacles in crossing the mountains from Carson to Placerville, snow having accumulated four feet deep during a storm which prevailed just previously. Only a narrow mule-path had been opened, and this was entirely occupied for miles by pack-trains on their way from California to the Washo mines. The express rider was compelled to dismount, and break a path around each mule met, thus causing several hours' delay."

New York **Times** *and Chicago* **Times**, *May 1, 1860.*

Even though Indian troubles and financial scandals grabbed the headlines, the weather caused the most problems, and eventually the downfall, of the Pony Express. The vast stretches of wilderness crossed by the pony riders were often swept by fierce storms and blanketed with deep snows—when it rained, there were miles of mudflats. William Russell promised that the mail could get through even in winter, but the winter of 1860-1861 tested the Pony Express to the utmost. Heavy snow fell all along the route. At first the riders could still get through following mule trains, but if there was no one to break the trail, the Pony Express came to a halt. Even when the trail was broken by mule traffic, it could still be hazardous. Tom King, a rider in western Wyoming, reported that if the rider was forced off the trail, "down you went belly deep to a horse, and perhaps deeper."

Nor was snow the only danger in winter. Howard Egan, station keeper and occasional rider in Division Four, once became snowblind. He was forced to lie in bed until an Indian, learning what had happened, offered to cure it for him. Anxious for any cure for his painful blindness, Egan agreed, whereupon the Indian put his mouth to Egan's eye and began to suck on his eyeball. Egan was unable to shake him off, and finally the Indian spit out a mouthful of blood and proceeded to do the same to Egan's other eye. The snowblindness was gone within two days.

In the Plains, there were violent thunderstorms with lightning and sheets of rain. When the snow melted in the Great Basin, the flat *playas* between mountain ranges turned into mudflats. Plagues of grasshoppers sometimes barred the way, or clouds of mosquitoes gave the riders another reason to change horses in a hurry. In spring, the big rivers the riders had to cross on the Plains were swollen with icy water, and there were few bridges. On the first ride, the Platte River was flooded near Julesburg, but the rider plunged in anyway. The horse was swept into quicksand, but the rider managed to save the *mochila* and swim to shore. Fortunately, there was a crowd of spectators, so the rider grabbed one of their horses and galloped away. The crowd gave him three cheers, and then, practical frontiersmen that they were, set about rescuing his horse.

Most of Nevada remains much as the Pony Express riders saw it in 1860. Although the trail and the station sites are marked and guidebooks are available, following the Pony Express route through central Nevada gives the modern traveler a real sense of what it was like to carry the mails through this wild country. Just like the Pony Express riders, if it snows, you can be stuck for days.

Often thought of as a hot desert plant, cactus such as this beautiful prickly pear can exist in much colder climates such as the high deserts of the Great Basin. Naturally, the Pony Express riders avoided such obstacles as much as they could!

"Sand-Springs Station deserved its name. Like the Brazas de San Diego and other **mauvaises terres** *near the Rio Grande, the land is cumbered here and there with drifted ridges of the finest sand, sometimes 200 feet high, and shifting before every gale.... The water near this vile hole was thick and stale with sulphury salts: it blistered even the hands. The station-house was no unfit object in such a scene, roofless and chairless, filthy and squalid, with a smoky fire in one corner, and a table in the centre of an impure floor, the walls open to every wind, and the interior full of dust."*

Sir Richard F. Burton, **The City of the Saints and Across the Rocky Mountains,** *1860.*

California, the Golden State, was the entire *raison d'être* of the Pony Express. The fastest ride ever made by the Pony Express was specifically to bring the text of President Lincoln's inaugural address to California in the shortest possible time. As the country began to tear apart in 1860, California was still undecided. There was strong sentiment for the South in California, and the southern states desperately craved the riches and political power that control of the state would bring. One of the originators of the Pony Express, California Senator William Gwin, was a southerner and later joined the Confederacy. Likewise, it was vital that the North keep California in the Union camp, and every effort was made through the Pony Express to bring this about.

The final leg of the westward bound Pony Express rider was much like the first leg in one respect. The route could still be difficult, especially crossing the towering Sierra Nevada mountains, but the route passed through country that had been settled since the first great influx of settlers and miners started in 1849, and near San Francisco, a century and more earlier. Civilization began at Dayton Station, just east of Carson City. Dayton was a product of the Comstock Lode gold rush of 1859, and at the time of the Pony Express had a population of 2,500 people. Next was Carson City, Nevada, today the capitol of Nevada. There was a Pony Express station on what is now Carson Street, and Bolivar Roberts, the division agent, had his headquarters there. From there, the riders began the long climb over the Sierras to the last station in Nevada, Friday's, or Lakeside Station, on the shores of Lake Tahoe. Friday's was a small town, with a two-story hostelry, and a roomy building that doubled as a stable and hay barn.

From Friday's, the riders passed into California. There were 15 stations between Carson City and Sacramento, most of them in the small towns that had grown since the Gold Rush of 1849. Sacramento was one of the most important stops for the Pony Express, and often it was the end of the line for the pony riders. Usually, the rider would gallop up to the docks on the Sacramento River and pass the *mochila* to the captain of the *Antelope,* one of the steamers that plied the river between San Francisco and Sacramento. If the rider missed the connection for any reason, he would continue on to the Benicia, Martinez, and Oakland stations before arriving at the true end of the line, the Pony Express offices at 153 Montgomery Street in San Francisco.

Built during the Pyramid Lake Indian War in 1860, Fort Churchill was for a brief time the terminus of the Overland Telegraph Company. Important news carried by the Pony Express would be telegraphed from there to San Francisco. Today, Fort Churchill is a Nevada state park.

Just about every traveler on the Pony Express and Overland Mail described Sand Springs as the worst station they encountered on the whole route, but the site was in use for ranching and agriculture until World War II. Today, it is listed on the National Register of Historic Places.

"St. Joseph, July 30—.... The route between Carson Valley and Salt Lake is now reported well stocked, and clear of Indians, so that future trips of the Express are expected regularly."

Chicago **Tribune**, *August 1, 1860.*

After the Pyramid Lake War, the Pony Express had difficulties getting back on track. Californians, having had a taste of rapid communications, clamored for the federal government to subsidize the Pony Express. Russell assured everyone that the mails would go through with or without the government subsidy, but when the bill supporting the subsidies failed to pass a Congress distracted by the secession crisis, he knew they were in trouble. Rumors started to circulate that the Pony Express was in financial trouble, and it was true—the Indian troubles in Utah and Nevada had cost the firm dearly. In late July, the station keepers along the route were issued 100 revolvers and 800 cartridges to help defend themselves. Yet another expense for William Waddell to enter into the debit column in his books!

No sooner had Russell gotten investors calmed down than Indian trouble once again flared in Utah and Nevada. On August 11, 1860, several hundred Indians assembled at Egan Canyon Station, west of Salt Lake City, demanding provisions and stealing the livestock. Just then, Lt. Stephen Weed's mounted patrol of U.S. Cavalry arrived at the station. He ordered his 25 troopers to attack, and the Indians fled without further battle. The next day, the same group of Indians attacked Schell Station, farther east, surrounding the station and driving off some of the livestock. The ubiquitous Lt. Weed, who later died bravely as a brigadier general of U.S. volunteers at Gettysburg, again saved the day, attacking and killing 17 of the warriors. Richard Burton describes meeting Lt. Weed and his troop, fresh from having "...done good service against the Gosh-Yutas." Even with army assistance from Camp Floyd and Ruby Valley, the Pony Express was forced to hire additional men to guard each station along this segment of the route, and fortify the stations with adobe and stone walls.

At the same time as the Egan Canyon incident, a group of Indians approached Deep Creek Station farther west. Warned off, they returned the next day and fired on the station, mortally wounding two of the staff. By the end of the summer, even the irrepressible William Russell was worried. The partners finally decided to keep the Pony Express in operation only until January 1861, especially after hearing a rumor that the federal government might not automatically renew their contract when it expired in November 1860.

Russell and his partners decided it was time for some good publicity. They arranged to carry the news of the November election—one of the most important ever to take place in the United States—between the two ends of the telegraph at Fort Kearny, Nebraska, and Fort Churchill, Nevada, in only five days. On November 7, 1860, a special Pony Express, the rider and horse decorated with ribbons, left for Salt Lake City. The news of Lincoln's election arrived there three days later, in spite of heavy snow, and the riders set out at once for Fort Churchill, arriving within the promised five days. The contract was renewed, and the Pony Express was back in business.

Many Mormons were already in California when the Gold Rush began in 1849, sent there by Brigham Young to establish way stations along the route to California. Mormon Station in Genoa, Nevada, was one of those, and is now protected as a Nevada state historic park.

Cottonwood trees, such as these along the Carson River in Nevada, only grow around a reliable source of water. While a good supply of water was essential for the Pony Express, standing water also meant that the station keepers and riders would be beset by mosquitoes during the warmer months.

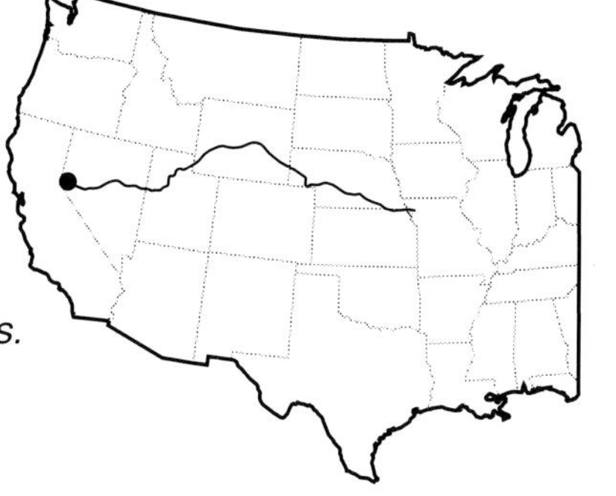

"The pony rider was usually a little bit of a man, brimful of spirit and endurance. No matter what time of day or night his watch came on, and no matter whether it was winter or summer, raining, snowing, hailing, or sleeting, or whether his 'beat' was a level straight road or a crazy trail over mountain craigs and precipices, or whether it led through peaceful regions or regions that swarmed with hostile Indians, he must be always ready to leap into the saddle and be off like the wind!"

Mark Twain, **Roughing It**, *1872.*

Even as the riders were struggling through deep snow in January 1861, the tangled web of finances that kept the Pony Express alive was beginning to unravel. Russell, Majors, and Waddell's financial troubles actually started years before the first rider set out, during the Utah War in the winter of 1857-58. The firm lost three complete wagon trains in Wyoming, burned by Mormon guerrillas. Already in debt for almost half a million dollars for those trains, the partners were unable to meet expenses and were only saved by a last-minute bail-out from the Secretary of War. They presented a large bill to the government in 1858, seeking redress for the loss, but it was never paid. When the army decided to send more men to Utah, the company had to supply them too. They were bound by the terms of their freighting contract to purchase 10 million pounds of supplies, and had to replace all equipment destroyed in the war.

Then the Pyramid Lake War erupted, and cost the firm thousands of dollars to replace equipment, rebuild stations, purchase new livestock, and hire extra guards for the stations in Utah and Nevada. Another problem was Russell himself, who couldn't resist starting new ventures even as the old ones were tottering. The firm was forced to bail out the Leavenworth and Pikes Peak Express Company, which Russell had started in 1859, when the expected freighting business to Denver failed to materialize. They also had their usual military supply contracts, for which they had to purchase goods and equipment on credit. When those trains didn't leave on schedule, the company had to pay for all those idle men and trains for several months.

Russell, Majors, and Waddell were depending on the successful performance of the Pony Express to induce the government to give them a lucrative contract to carry the overland mail, but the Indian wars and the weather finished that hope. Congress, distracted by the secession crisis, adjourned without passing a bill establishing a central overland mail route—and Russell, Majors, and Waddell were left with a mountain of debt, contracts they were obligated to fulfill, and no hope of any regular income.

Once the Pony Express riders left the deserts of Utah and Nevada, the next challenge was the crossing of the mighty Sierra Nevada. A difficult journey even in the summer, in the winter, when deep snow choked the trails, the crossing could be deadly.

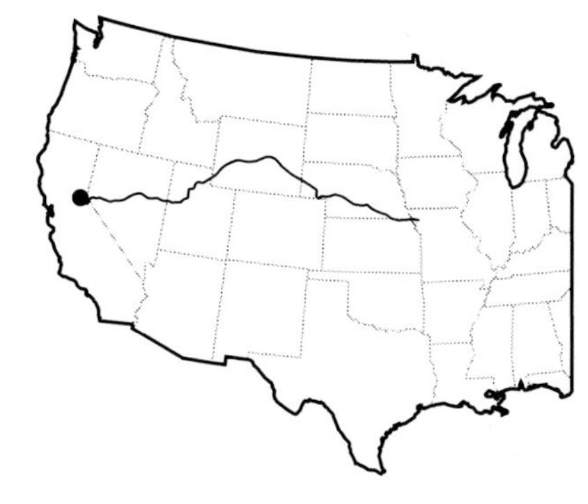

Yank's Station was the first one in California that the westbound Pony Express riders reached, and being near the crest of the Sierra Nevada it was also one of the highest. Snow around the station could completely cover the buildings in winter.

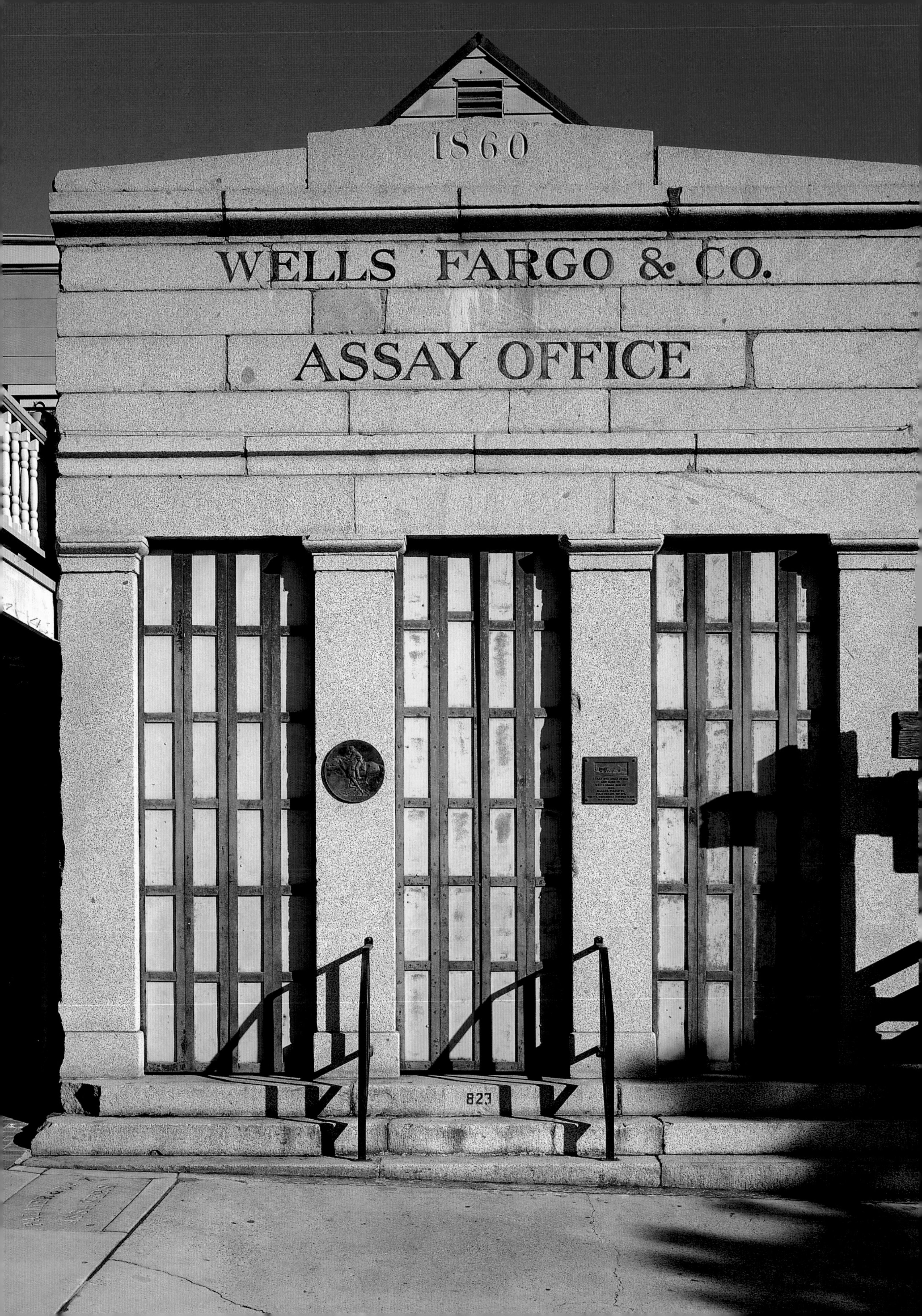
1860
WELLS FARGO & CO.
ASSAY OFFICE
823

*"***Suspension of the Pony Express***—Wells, Fargo & Company, having received a dispatch from the East, directing the stopping of the Pony Express, that active animal may be considered as withdrawn from the Overland course.* **Peace to his manes!"**

San Francisco **Alta California,** *October 27, 1861.*

Finally, in obvious desperation, Russell turned to outright fraud. Obtaining Indian trust bonds from a relative of Secretary of War John Floyd, Russell took them to New York, passed them off as his own, and secured large loans against them. When he was confronted by the need to return the bonds, which he couldn't do, instead of coming clean he "borrowed" a further set of bonds and got more loans! Knowing he had no money to back them up, Russell had become an embezzler, but amazingly, he again got away with it. Then Godard Bailey, the man who had loaned Russell the bonds, had an attack of conscience and confessed to their schemes in a letter to the Secretary of War. Bailey was immediately arrested, and federal marshals arrested Russell at his home in New York City on Christmas Eve, 1860.

News of the bond scandal caused an immediate sensation in the whole country. Blame in the case was evenly spread—Russell's detractors brought up his reputation for shady deals, while his supporters declared that it was the government's fault, for not paying Russell, Majors, and Waddell for their losses in the Utah War. Russell was indicted in January 1861 for fraud, but was saved from prosecution by the approach of the Civil War. After South Carolina seceded in December 1860, William Russell's peculations didn't seem very important, and the indictment was quashed.

Russell, Majors, and Waddell were haunted by lawsuits filed by angry creditors for the rest of their lives. Russell, once the "Napoleon of the West," tried one scheme after another to recoup his shattered fortunes, but was finally reduced to selling patent neuralgia medicine on the streets of New York. When his health began to fail, his family brought him back to Missouri, where he died on September 10, 1872, at 60 years of age. Waddell weathered the bond scandal best of all. Even though he had to sell all of his property and never again was trusted in business, he sold his large house in Lexington, Missouri, to his son for $1.00 so he could continue to live there for the rest of his life. He died on April 1, 1872. Alexander Majors, who outlived the other two by almost 30 years, was also ruined by the scandal. He tried to return to freighting for a few years after the Pony Express collapsed, but moved to Salt Lake City in 1867, to work on grading the roadbed for the transcontinental railroad. He was present when the Golden Spike was driven at Promontory on May 10, 1869. After failing as a prospector, he sank into obscurity until Buffalo Bill Cody found him living alone in a shack near Denver, writing his memoirs. Cody paid to have the manuscript edited and published under the title *Seventy Years on the Frontier.* Alexander Majors died in Chicago on January 14, 1900.

Ironically, the financial collapse of Russell, Majors, and Waddell came about just as the Pony Express was reaching its stride—use of the Pony Express actually increased as the lines of the telegraph crept closer together. The Pony Express was more important than ever in the spring of 1861, as each new *mochila* brought eagerly awaited news of the battles then raging in the East.

Sportsman's Hall, about 50 miles east of Sacramento, was the only Pony Express home station in California. Built as a hotel in 1852, it was a busy place. During the Comstock Lode boom of 1859, as many as seven stages per day passed by its doors.

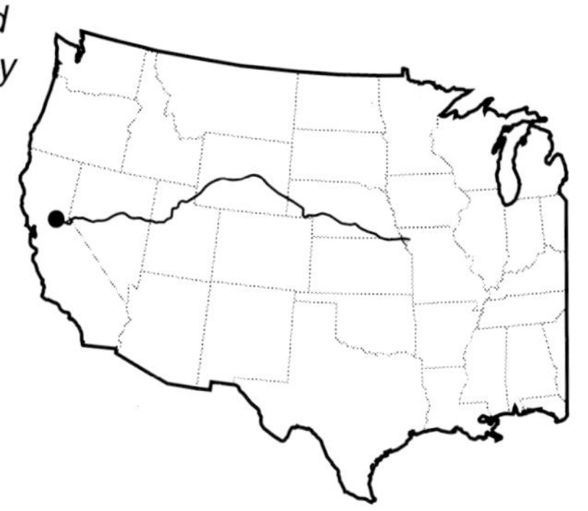

The Wells Fargo office in Folsom, California, briefly served as the western terminus of the Pony Express. From there, the mail would be carried on the Sacramento Valley Railroad to Sacramento. In July 1861, the western terminus of the Pony Express was moved to Placerville, California.

B. F. HASTINGS & CO.
SUPREME COURT
WELLS, FARGO & Co.

"Pony Express Notice—Orders having been received from W. H. Russell, President Pony Express Company, I hereby transfer the office and everything pertaining thereto to Messrs. Wells, Fargo & Co. All letters to be forwarded by Pony Express must be delivered at their office on Second Street, between J and K, Sacramento. J. W. Coleman, Agent Pony Express Co."

Sacramento Union, *May 16, 1861.*

The bond scandal ruined the firm of Russell, Majors, and Waddell, but the firm that actually ran the Pony Express—the Central Overland California and Pikes Peak Express Company—was a separate corporation. The Pony Express continued to operate under its original management as if nothing had happened. Support for the Pony Express came from residents of California, who needed it now more than ever. The central route used by the Pony Express was still unproven, given the problems with both Indian tribes and the weather. At this late date there were still people in the country who insisted that a southern route, through Texas, New Mexico, and Arizona to southern California, was preferable. But when Texas seceded in February 1861, and Confederate forces stopped the stagecoaches, it was obvious that for the foreseeable future, the central route was the only option.

In March 1861, mail service along the southern route was officially ended, and the contract for mail and passenger service was split, giving the Overland Mail Company the western half of the line, from California to Salt Lake City. The eastern half, from St. Joseph to Salt Lake City, was given to the Central Overland California and Pikes Peak Express Company, since the Overland Mail Company couldn't afford to operate the entire line. In exchange for the loss of the western half of the line, Congress agreed to subsidize the Pony Express until the transcontinental telegraph was completed.

The two companies divided the receipts from the Pony Express. Amazingly, given the breaking bond scandal, Russell was given the contract for the Central Overland California and Pikes Peak Express Company to run the mails on the eastern half of the line. It was his last act as a director of the firm—on April 26, 1861, Russell, in full light of the bond scandal, was asked to resign, thus ending his involvement with the Pony Express. In spring of 1861, responsibility for the western half of the Pony Express was turned over to the Overland Mail Company, which promptly turned it over to Wells Fargo. Well Fargo was already well known for carrying freight, passengers, and mail, but mostly in California. They carried the mails until July 1, 1861, when Ben Holladay's Overland Mail Company took over completely. On October 24, 1861, the lines of the telegraph met in Salt Lake City, and with that meeting came the end of the Pony Express. Even though the last *mochila* wasn't delivered until November, as soon as the first transcontinental messages hummed along the "talking wires," the Pony Express passed into history and legend.

This sculpture of a Pony Express rider outside the B. F. Hastings Building in Sacramento, California, is one of six in the nation. Other statues honoring the Pony Express are in St. Joseph, Missouri; Marysville, Kansas; Salt Lake City, Utah; and Reno, Nevada; and at Harrah's Casino in Stateline, Nevada.

The B. F. Hastings Building is one of Sacramento's most historic buildings. Originally built in 1853, it served as the home of the California Supreme Court and the offices of Wells Fargo, housed California's first telegraph company, and was the official western terminus of the Pony Express. The building has been restored and today is a California historic site.

"MEN WANTED! The undersigned wishes to hire ten or a dozen men, familiar with the management of horses, as hostlers, or riders on the Overland Express Route via Salt Lake City. Wages $50 per month and found."

Sacramento **Union**, *March 19, 1860.*

It's only human nature that almost as soon as the ponies stopped running, men began to step forward—enough for a regiment, even though there were never more than 80 riders—and claim that they were one of the riders. As Mark Twain said about meeting agent Jack Slade, "Here was romance, and I was sitting face to face with it!" And what young man could resist basking in the glow of romance, even if only dimly reflected? The one who comes first to the public's mind is Buffalo Bill Cody, although there's some doubt as to whether he was a rider. No matter—he thought he was, and convinced everyone of his day that he was. He was also the leader in promoting the myth of the Pony Express through his Wild West show.

Not that there weren't authentic heroes. "Pony Bob" Haslam once rode almost 200 miles during the Pyramid Lake War when his relief refused to leave the safety of the station. He returned over the same route the next day, dodging war parties of Paiutes and Shoshones, only to find the station looted and the keeper dead. Or how about Jay Kelley, station keeper in Nevada? When the rider came in mortally wounded by Indians and died soon after, Kelley—the lightest man at the station—took over as the rider without a second thought. Even the wives of station keepers and riders were forced to be resourceful, if not heroic—Mary Faylor, wife of rider Josiah Faylor, once found herself alone when Indians came to the station. To make them think she wasn't alone, she put hats and caps on sticks and placed these near the windows so it would look like the men were home.

But when it comes to the Wild West, America has always loved its scoundrels as well as its heroes, and there were scoundrels in the Pony Express. Many of the station keepers and riders in the more isolated stations were there for the anonymity that the frontier provided. There was Jules Reni, the whiskey-guzzling leader of an outlaw gang, station keeper in Colorado, later killed by Jack Slade; Slade himself, agent of Division Two, who ended his checkered career at the end of a rope in Montana; and William Carr, a rider in Nevada who murdered Bernard Chessy in cold blood in 1860, and gained the dubious honor of being the guest of honor at Nevada's first legal execution.

Some Pony Express employees skated along the edges of the law. Wild Bill Hickok worked as a stocktender in Nebraska, and went on to gain fame as a gunman and sheriff. He was shot to death while playing poker in a Deadwood, South Dakota, saloon. Porter Rockwell, the mysterious keeper of Rockwell's Station south of Salt Lake City, was reputed to be a leader of the Sons of Dan—the Danites, or Mormon Militia—known to all westerners of the day as the Avenging Angels. Rockwell was a bodyguard to Brigham Young, and reportedly swore blood revenge on the Governor of Missouri for the murder of Mormon Prophet Joseph Smith.

What happened to the riders and station keepers? Howard Egan, agent in Utah and Nevada, died in 1878 after he "took sick" guarding Brigham Young's grave one stormy night. Rider Samuel Gilson prospected all over the West, and discovered an important mineral, Gilsonite, in eastern Utah. "Kootenai" Brown, another rider, was instrumental in establishing Glacier National Park. Others enlisted on both sides in the Civil War—many, like Johnny Frye, never returned. Thomas Ranahan and many others became scouts during the Indian wars that swept the West after the Civil War. A few capitalized on their fame, like Buffalo Bill; four became Mormon bishops, while others went on to careers in business, ranching, and politics. Billy Campbell, one of the youngest riders, was also the last; he died in 1932 at the age of 90. No matter the course of their later lives, whether they died under a blaze of gunfire, or lived to a ripe, respected old age, not a one of them ever forgot their time with the Pony Express.

ST. JOSEPH MUSEUM, ST. JOSEPH, MISSOURI

The statues and memorials honoring the riders of the Pony Express, and the few remaining photographs—taken during an infrequent night out on the town—are about the only things that are definite about the riders. Some few went on to abiding fame or lasting infamy. Others lived out their lives in the quiet obscurity of the frontier. Many vanished from the pages of history altogether.

"Latest news BY TELEGRAPH. Per Pony Express. San Francisco, May 29. The overland telegraph expedition left Sacramento on the 27th, for Carson Valley, at which point they are to commence laying wires towards Salt Lake. The expedition embraces 228 head of oxen, 26 wagons, and 50 men."

Leavenworth Daily Times,
June 11, 1861.

WYOMING DIVISION OF CULTURAL RESOURCES

The crews constructing the Overland Telegraph used the same route as the riders of the Pony Express, so it was only natural that when the wires were joined in Salt Lake City in October 1861—officially ending the Pony Express—many of the stations were taken over by the men who maintained the "talking wires."

Evening  Bulletin.

VOL. XII. SAN FRANCISCO. WEDNESDAY EVENING. JUNE 12. 1861.

to be entrenched, mounted with rifled cannon, well fortified and kept under strict martial law. The different arms of the service—infantry, cavalry and artillery—will each be put through a regular course of instruction, lines of pickets and scouts will be thrown out so as to prevent the approach to camp of any improper persons, and the military discipline of the men will be perfect in every respect.

The California regiment under Col. Matheson, received on Thursday three addi... and is expected to be...

notice. From the face which this gentleman makes at being obliged to define his position in these trying times, there is good reason for believing that, notwithstanding his oath to the contrary, he is a Secessionist at heart. His affiliation with the Brothers Wood's organ is almost enough to prove this.

The Late Seizure of Telegraphic Despatches.

In my last letter I referred hurriedly to the ...seizure at all the telegraph offices in ...which had

their destinies with those of a Southern Confederacy. How the first blast of the Northern bugle has blown away these bubbles of the imagination!

No Dependence on the Loyalty of Maryland.

A telegram to the *Tribune* dated Washington, May 24th says:

The pretended Union sentiment of Baltimore is not to be trusted. The Government has information of the most direct and positive character, which shows that United States troops alone keep the city in order. The Administration has satisfied ...there has existed a conspiracy against ...leading cit...

LETTER FROM FORT YUMA.

[FROM AN OCCASIONAL CORRESPONDENT.]

FORT YUMA, CAL., May 30, 1861.

I would direct the attention of the U. S. Postal Agent at San Francisco to the carelessness and inefficiency which impairs even the unsatisfactory privilege of a semi-monthly communication with civilization, to which, since the withdrawal of the Overland Mail by this route, we have been reduced. In this all-pervading atmosphere of excitement, which begets a fevered impatience at any delay in ...mission of the eventful news which crowds

A Poor Show for California Emigrants to the Nez Perces Mines.

The *Oregonian*, (Portland) of the 1st of June says:

The *Julia* on her last trip carried up a large number of miners and their supplies. When we witness this movement of our people, we cannot but think of the past. This is the eighth gold excitement in Oregon. We have not become permanently better off for either of them; and some of them have been disastrous to our people. We believe there is gold at the new mines—and, so there is at Colville, Wenatchee, Pen d'Oreille, Rock Creek and other points on our frontiers. The publications made in regard to the Nez Perces mines, are but the revised editions of the accounts of other mines that at this time do not attract the crowd. ...lieving that there is no gold at ...think there is, and a good ...be made there at ...strikes. The ...times ...we

therefore, be found to have really had ... in it."

List of Pony Express Letters.

The Pony Express will arrive here to-night, by the steamer from Sacramento, bringing letters addressed to the following persons in this city:

W. H. Watson,
Barron & Co.,
James Eldridge,
J. Cohen & Co.,
George F. Bragg,
DeWitt Kittle & Co.,
Kerby, Byrne & Co.,
Joseph Genella,
Dickson, De Wolf & Co.,
White & Wilson,
Smiley, Yerkes & Co.,
John Winter,
H. Applegate,
William Newell & Co.,
Mary Dempsey,
Bachman Bros.,
W. B. Vandyke,
G. W. Guthrie,
Echo du Pacifique,
C. H. Burton,
W. B. Cummings & Co.,
Alexander Leikauff,
David P. Belknap,
William Walsh,
Evening Bulletin,
John S. Hittell,
William Booth,
Neustadter Bros.,
J. Neale Plumb,
W. J. Hartman,
Eppinger & Co.,
William Faulkner,
J. G. Eastman,
M. Weller & Bros.,
Stanford Bros.,
George Stevens,
Jesse Halladay,
J. B. Newton & Co.,
Mrs. James Stanton,
Haggin & Tevis,
Tubbs & Co.,
Atta,
Thomas Smiley & Co.,
Samuel Knight,
Forbes & Babcock,
J. Y. Hallock & Co.,
H. Cohen & Co.,
Conroy & O'Conner,
Edward Seaman,
Frank Baker,
Wm. H. Coddington,
Eugene Casserly,
Levi Strauss,
Taylor & Swasey,
Falkner, Bell & Co.,
J. H. Coghill & Co.,
C. W. Brooks & Co.,
W. Alvord & Co.,
Hoffin & Rosenstock,
R. S. Eells,
I. B. Purdy & Co.

Doings at Virginia—The Disunionists Checkmated.

A correspondent of the *Bulletin*, writing from Virginia City, N. T., on Saturday evening, the 8th

and letters will ...
The N. Y. *Post* ...
says, preparations are ...
movement of the Gove...
all under arms, and are rea...
ment's notice. The probable ...
concentration upon the rebel fo...
A party of 50 rebels had rea...
Harper's Ferry; they are ...
Cadwalader has an eye on them...
The N. Y. *Tribune's* Washin...
says all is quiet at Fortress M...
were at the fortress, and the nu...
The Washington *Star* says ...
at Sewall's Point in the recent ...
the rebels had stopped work o...
at Manassas.
15,000 soldiers were concen...
Virginia.
Four companies of the Di...
crossed into Virginia with six d...
In the Wheeling District the U...
1,300 majority. In the Parkers...
WASHINGTON, May 31.—Ja...
has been appointed Envoy Ext...
istor Plenipotentiary to Brazil.
The Revenue laws require ves...
with informal papers to be se...
as those coming from the South...
houses are in possession of insu...
and they cannot obtain the pr...
Secretary of the Treasury, with...
ing the embarrassment and tr...
cumstances, has decided that ...
appears that there was no faul...
commander, the latter shall not...
into court; but on a correct re...
Collector where the vessels arriv...
shall be remitted.

Epilogue

The Pony Express lasted just 18 months. The riders made 308 rides each way—a distance of 616,000 miles—carrying almost 35,000 pieces of mail. By any standards of business, it was a miserable failure. Despite the heroic efforts of the riders and station keepers, not to mention the considerable skills of the three partners, the harsh reality of weather and the rising tide of Indian anger overwhelmed the Pony Express. When it ended on October 26, 1861, the Central Overland California and Pikes Peak Express Company was over $400,000 in debt, its equipment and stations worn out and run down, and its creditors from Missouri to California worried about receiving payment. The failure of the Pony Express brought about the financial and personal ruin of William Russell, Alexander Majors, and William Waddell.

But there is much more to the Pony Express than just figures in the books of Russell, Majors, and Waddell. Thousands of businesses have started, flourished, and disappeared in America, and have left no more mark on history than a record in an obscure, dusty archive. Yet today people the world over recognize the icon of the rider on the galloping horse. The Pony Express, no matter what its profits and losses, has made some very real contributions to American history, then and now, both tangible and spiritual.

Most tangible was its effect in pulling the two ends of the nation together at one of the most critical periods in American history. Just as the forces of secession threatened to pull it apart, the Pony Express, "like a weaver's shuttle back and forth," stitched it back together. "We have looked to you as those who wait for the morning, and how seldom did you fail us!" the editor of the *California Pacific* wrote. All through the tense summer of 1861, the pony riders brought news of great battles, stirring speeches in Congress, calls for volunteers, and the lists of dead, wounded, and missing to anxious westerners. Modern historians may argue whether the Pony Express kept California in the Union, but to the people at the time there was no doubt.

There were other immediate, palpable effects as well. The news carried by the pony riders helped move the Mormons back into the mainstream of American culture and politics. Just two years before, Utah had been besieged by a federal army bent on destroying the New Jerusalem on the shore of the Great Salt Lake. By the time the pony riders stopped coming, Utah was a solid, if sometimes reluctant, participant in the great American experiment. The pony riders also served vital local functions, giving warning of Indian troubles, and spreading news among the isolated towns and settlements along the route. And until the financial structure began to fail, working for the Pony Express provided hard cash to struggling ranchers and merchants for 2,000 miles across an unsettled wilderness.

Another effect is not so tangible but is much more durable. The daring young riders of the Pony Express became the perfect symbol for the myth of the American frontier: brave and self-reliant, they showed a can-do spirit that Americans have always felt was

How did people know when they had received mail via the Pony Express? Newspapers in every city along the route would obtain a list of the letters in the mailbag when the "Pony" came in, and then publish the names in the newspaper. People who had mail could then go to the local office and pick up their letters.

No fewer than 23 museums are dedicated wholly or in part to the Pony Express in Missouri, Kansas, Nebraska, Colorado, Wyoming, Utah, Nevada, and California. Many other museums in those same states, and in other places, bring alive the history of the Pony Express through exhibits, publications, and dioramas such as this replica of the inside of the Patee House.

PONY EXPRESS!

CHANGE OF TIME!

REDUCED RATES!

10 Days to San Francisco!

LETTERS

WILL BE RECEIVED AT THE

OFFICE, 84 BROADWAY,

NEW YORK,

Up to 4 P. M. every TUESDAY,

AND

Up to 2½ P. M. every SATURDAY,

Which will be forwarded to connect with the PONY EXPRESS leaving ST. JOSEPH, Missouri,

Every WEDNESDAY and SATURDAY at 11 P. M.

TELEGRAMS

Sent to Fort Kearney on the mornings of MONDAY and FRIDAY, will connect with **PONY** leaving St. Joseph, WEDNESDAYS and SATURDAYS.

EXPRESS CHARGES.

LETTERS weighing half ounce or under............$1 00
For every additional half ounce or fraction of an ounce 1 00
In all cases to be enclosed in 10 cent Government Stamped Envelopes,

And all Express CHARGES Pre-paid.

☞ PONY EXPRESS ENVELOPES For Sale at our Office.

WELLS, FARGO & CO., Ag'ts.

New York, July 1, 1861.

SLOTE & JANES, STATIONERS AND PRINTERS, 93 FULTON STREET, NEW YORK.

REPRESENTATIVE COMPOSITE OF PONY EXPRESS ADVERTISEMENT: NEVADA HISTORICAL SOCIETY

their birthright. As one writer has said, "Speed is an American virtue"—and what better exemplifies speed than the Pony Express? Even though the idea of a pony express is ancient, and pony riders are known the world over, the Pony Express can never be anything but an American story.

Interest in the Pony Express is if anything greater today than it was during its brief appearance on the world stage. Hundreds of books and articles have been written about it; stage plays, radio dramas, and motion pictures have recreated the sights and sounds of the dashing riders. There are monuments, museums, postage stamps, reenactment societies, and anniversary celebrations. The National Pony Express Association has hundreds of members worldwide. Not bad for a handful of riders and station keepers on the lonely frontier—entire nations have left less of a mark on history.

SUGGESTED READING

Reading the classics on the subject will give a special sense of the myth, romanticism, and reality of the Pony Express.

BLOSS, ROY S. *Pony Express—The Great Gamble.* Berkeley, California: Howell-North Publishers, 1959.

BRADLEY, GLENN D. *The Story of the Pony Express.* Chicago: A. C. McClurg & Company, 1913.

CHAPMAN, ARTHUR. *The Pony Express: The Record of a Romantic Adventure in Business.* New York: G. P. Putnam's Sons, 1932.

DRIGGS, HOWARD R. *The Pony Express Goes Through: An American Saga Told by Its Heroes.* New York: Frederick A. Stokes Company, 1935.

SETTLE, RAYMOND W. and MARY L. SETTLE. *Empire on Wheels.* Stanford, California: Stanford University Press, 1949.

SETTLE, RAYMOND W. and MARY L. SETTLE. *Saddles and Spurs: The Pony Express Saga.* Harrisburg, Pennsylvania: The Stackpole Company, 1955.

SETTLE, RAYMOND W. and MARY L. SETTLE. *War Drums and Wagon Wheels: The Story of Russell, Majors, and Waddell.* Lincoln: University of Nebraska Press, 1966.

For an annotated bibliography of these works and others, see:

GODFREY, ANTHONY. *Historic Resource Study: Pony Express National Historic Trail.* Washington, D.C.: Government Printing Office, 1994.

Books in the "Voyage of Discovery" series: California Trail, Lewis & Clark, Mormon Trail, Oregon Trail, Pony Express, John Wesley Powell, Santa Fe Trail. Also available is a book on the Oregon Trail Center near Baker City, Oregon. Selected titles in this series can be ordered with a booklet in German or Spanish bound into the center of the English book.

To receive our catalog with over 115 titles:

Call (800-626-9673), fax (702-433-3420), write to the address below, Or visit our web site at www.kcpublications.com

Published by KC Publications, 3245 E. Patrick Ln., Suite A, Las Vegas, NV 89120.

Created, Designed, and Published in the U.S.A.
Ink formulated by Daihan Ink Co., Ltd.
Printed by Doosan Corporation, Seoul, Korea
Color Separations by Kedia/Kwang Yang Sa Co., Ltd.
Paper produced exclusively by Hankuk Paper Mfg. Co., Ltd.